The Autobiography of

POPS FOSTER

New Orleans Jazzman

The Autobiography of

POPS FOSTER

New Orleans Jazzman

as told to Tom Stoddard

Interchapters by Ross Russell

Backbeat
Books
San Francisco

Published by Backbeat Books
600 Harrison Street, San Francisco, CA 94107
www.backbeatbooks.com
email: books@musicplayer.com

An imprint of CMP Information
Publishers of *Guitar Player*, *Bass Player*, *Keyboard*, and *EQ* magazines

CMP
United Business Media

Distributed to the book trade in the US and Canada by
Publishers Group West, 1700 Fourth Street, Berkeley, CA 94710

Distributed to the music trade in the US and Canada by
Hal Leonard Publishing, P.O. Box 13819, Milwaukee, WI 53213

Cover design by Richard Leeds—www.bigwigdesign.com
Composition by Maureen Forys, Happenstance Type-O-Rama
Photos are from the author's collection, courtesy of Loretta Stoddard, with the
    following exceptions:
    Frontispiece: the last photo taken of Pops Foster, March 1969, later mounted
        on his headstone. Courtesy of Ed Lawless.
    Page xxv courtesy of International Society of Bassists.
    Page 24 courtesy of Karl Gert zer Heide.
    Page 26 courtesy of Archives of New Orleans Jazz, Tulane University.
    Page 161 courtesy of Ed Lawless.

Library of Congress Cataloging-in-Publication Data

Foster, Pops, 1892–1969.
   [Pops Foster]
The autobiography of Pops Foster : New Orleans jazzman, as told to Tom Stoddard /
[Foreword to the new edition by Ron Carter; introduction by Bertram Turetzky].
      p. cm.
Includes bibliographical references (p. 206), discography (p. 204), and index.
ISBN 0-87930-831-1 (alk. paper)
1. Foster, Pops, 1892–1969. 2. Jazz musicians—Biography. I. Stoddard, Tom.
II. Title.

   ML419.F68A3 2005
   787.5'165'092—dc22
                                              2004029269

Printed in the United States of America

05 06 07 08 09   5 4 3 2 1

Contents

Preface

꧁꧂

One of the best periods of my life began in May 1967; that was when I met George Murphy "Pops" Foster. At our first meeting, my wife, Roberta, and I were accompanied by our four children. Pops fell in love with them as he did with all children. A few weeks later Pops and Alma Foster came to our house for dinner, and a deep friendship developed. Pops wanted to tell what he knew of jazz after spending seven decades as a bass player, from the very beginnings of that musical form until the late 1960s. I agreed to set it to paper for him.

While the problems of writing such a book were few and the pleasures many, it seems worthwhile to recount some of the things that went into it in order to give the reader a better understanding of the book's limitations, emphasis, and construction.

My original plan was not to have a plan at all. I merely took my tape recorder to Pops's house and simply had him tell his story, only prompting him here and there with questions. I foolishly thought I could then transcribe the tape directly into a finished book. This method proved suitable for collecting a lot of basic material, but was, of course, completely inadequate for anything else. This first stage finally resulted in about 70 hours of taped interviews that will eventually be donated to an archive so as to make these tapes available to other researchers. The tapes were practically all made at Pops's house at 427 Webster Street in San Francisco. I would generally spend two to three hours at a time recording about one-and-a-half hours of tape. If I live to be as old as Pops, I doubt I will ever know more pleasant hours than these. Extracting and putting the material into final shape was a bitch of a job, and one on which I procrastinated far too long.

In the quiet of my home, with four raucous children, a 200-pound collie dog, and a wife who felt lonely whenever I put the tapes on, I began transcribing. After a slow start, I began to extract material by topical groupings. Whenever Pops started a new topic I left a blank line or two on the sheet. This method resulted in a pile of several hundred sheets of 8½-by-11-inch paper accumulating over almost two years. I then tore the sheets along the blank lines on the paper and grouped these into several large categories (McCall Plantation, New Orleans, the Riverboats and St. Louis, and a pile I called "way late"). The McCall material was very modest, but that became the first chapter and was easy to keep separate. The New Orleans material was about 30 percent of the whole and was the most difficult to thread together. As you will note, the material is arranged in roughly chronological order.

While transcribing the material from the tapes, I soon noted that Pops covered the same material a number of times and that the versions differed in some details. Usually, I felt I understood Pops and knew the story well enough to decide which was the most accurate version, and in all cases I tried to keep most of the details. Some seriously conflicting stories did come up, such as the time and place of Pops's last playing date with Freddie Keppard. In two or three instances it was at a banquet (pronounced "bonkay" by Pops), while at other times he remembered it as a parade with a brass band. In a number of instances I decided to leave both versions in the book, feeling that Pops erred only in the chronology, not in the actual occurrences. On other conflicting details, I consulted with Pops to check his story. I believe, however, the reader has what is probably the most accurate possible version of what happened.

The above is not intended to reflect in any way on Pops's memory. He was a very articulate man and had a most remarkable recall. He conjured up facts, details, names, and dates of events more than 60 years in the past with an ease that still evokes my admiration.

Pops's amazing recollection of the early jazz era is justification enough for this book. He had read and heard so much crap and claptrap about New Orleans and early jazz that he wanted to put the record straight, as he knew it. He wanted to title the book "The Whole Truth about New Orleans." It was this simple but profound desire to get the story straight that made him devote so much time and effort to it. This, I might mention, was not the first attempt to have him tell his story, but all the others somehow never came to fruition.

The reader will note on the opening pages that I have made a sincere effort to retell the book as Pops told it. The colloquial language is retained, the interesting phraseology and syntax are kept, and as many musical, folk, and regional expressions as possible have been left intact.

Knowing that readers would be interested in certain important personalities, I asked many questions about them. Thus, these individuals loom large in the book. Had the questions not been asked they probably would not have received as much attention. Ideally, it would have been interesting to put down only those things that came naturally to Pops's mind, without prompting him at all. It is, of course, too late now, and Jelly Roll Morton, Buddy Bolden, and others may be cut a shade larger than life.

The book contains virtually all the material collected on the tapes. I have tried to work that material into a fairly free-flowing book; however, I have not been altogether successful in this task. A number of details that may be of importance to the jazz historian have been put in the book even though they may interrupt the flow of the narrative. For these lapses in reading pleasure, I apologize.

I expect to be deluged with correspondence regarding inaccuracies and errors. I realize that many things in the book conflict with "known" jazz history. But Pops was a historical source and was as entitled to say his piece as the cat who wrote that history. Frankly, after spending all that time with Pops, I would be inclined to accept his version of the story. There probably will be a number of points that I may have misunderstood or where Pops was just plain wrong. Anyone who thinks so may certainly write. I do not promise to answer all the letters.

Finally, I would like to thank Pops and Alma Foster for their patience and understanding, and for lots of snacks and coffee. Thanks to my wife, Roberta, and my four children—Antigone, Hillary, Marcus, and Jana—for putting up with me during the two-and-a-half years of this project. Several people also deserve my thanks for helping with the book: Bertram Turetzky for the excellent critical analysis of Pops's career; Ross Russell for the sparkling interchapters; Alain Hénon for superb editing; Brian Rust for his great reference book, *Jazz Records 1897–1931*; Sam Charters for his book *Jazz New Orleans 1895–1963: An Index to the Negro Musicians of New Orleans*; and Joline DuBois for typing the manuscript. Thanks to these and the many others who helped and encouraged me.

—*Tom Stoddard*
San Anselmo, California
1971

Stoddard checks a galley prior to the 1971 publication of the first edition.

Foreword to
the New Edition

by Ron Carter

T he *Autobiography of Pops Foster* by the late Tom Stoddard takes us from the very beginning (his playing on a homemade string bass) to the death in 1969 of one of the first major string-bass performers and personalities. By using Mr. Foster's own colorful language in describing his early life and long years as a professional jazz musician, Stoddard allows us to smell the coffee, see the flowers, and stroll through the plantations, watching the seeds being planted and starting to grow that eventually produced Mr. Foster's fabulous and varied career. However, this autobiography is much more than a history of jazz and its early practitioners. It is an insider's view of society as it was during the first half of the 20th century, as observed and described and experienced by Mr. Foster: from the noted prohibitionist Carrie Nation's crusade, to the separation of the races, to the more subtle divisions by skin color within the black community, to the establishment of the segregated Musicians Union.

In a particularly interesting section of Mr. Foster's narration of his life, he offers details that confirm the now legendary story about the first jazz recording. Trumpeter Freddie Keppard was originally offered a recording contract by the Victor Talking Machine Company, but, fearing that other musicians would steal his musical ideas after they were recorded, he refused, opening the door for the Original Dixieland Jazz

Band. That's why the distinction of having made the first jazz recording, on February 24, 1917, in New York City, belongs to that group of white musicians led by Nick La Rocca. This and many other important historical musical facts are a vital part of Foster's autobiography.

Mr. Foster's memory of dates and personnel is truly astonishing. As a friend and occasional enemy, he crossed paths with the leading jazz musicians of the era; as a performance and recording partner, he worked with such luminaries as Sidney Bechet, Louis Armstrong, Lil Hardin Armstrong, Fletcher and Horace Henderson, Earl Hines, Kid Ory, Oran "Hot Lips" Page, Luis Russell, and Duke Ellington. These were just a few of the giants of jazz who felt and heard the swing and power of Foster's beat.

The lively description and compelling imagery of the life of a jazz musician, both on and off the bandstand, as recalled by Mr. Foster makes one feel like a witness to the events related and personalities described: the rivalry among musicians, the jealousies surrounding parts of their social life, the various types and locations of their gigs, the constant travel. It is easy to see how Mr. Stoddard became enthralled by Pops Foster's account of his life and his music. I certainly am.

—Ron Carter
2004

After rising to prominence with the Miles Davis Quintet in the 1960s, virtuoso soloist and sideman Ron Carter has gone on to become one of the most recorded bassists in the history of jazz. His discography includes more than 30 recordings of his own.

Introduction

by Bertram Turetzky

꧁꧂

The career of George "Pops" Foster is staggering to contemplate, as it ranges from Congo Square to John Coltrane—some 70 years. Foster was the first famous double-bass player in jazz, and he worked with almost all of the greats, including Louis Armstrong, Sidney Bechet, Duke Ellington, Earl Hines, and Charlie Parker. The only other double bassist to rival his career was Domenico Dragonetti (1763–1846), the Paganini of the contrabasso, who was the first celebrated European bass virtuoso. During Dragonetti's professional career of 69 years, he became a friend of Haydn and Beethoven, among others. Both Foster and Dragonetti represent, historically speaking, the beginning of a growing awareness of the importance of the double bass in African-American jazz and European concert music, and both had careers of prodigious length. Both maintained a dazzling performance level from their genesis to their last days, and both left important legacies.

Foster, one of the handful of string bassists[1] to gain a place on the bandstand for the double bass in the days of the legendary Buddy Bolden, developed musically through the 1920s and 1930s and was still able to bowl over thousands of aficionadi at the 1963 Monterey

---

1. A term used in the early 1900s to differentiate between wind and bass (i.e. tuba) and the contrabass or double bass.

Jazz Festival at the age of 72! Around that time he worked in a quartet with Richard Hadlock, soprano sax; Elmer Snowden, banjo and guitar; and a "swing" drummer doubling vibes. They played a repertoire ranging from ragtime and Jelly Roll Morton pieces to Thelonious Monk tunes. Pops never faltered, and more important, never lost his own wonderful identity.[2]

The love of music and quest for knowledge permeated his entire life. This is one of the reasons why he outswung and outlived so many of his contemporaries. "I used to pick up ideas from everybody. Sometimes I would find an alley guitar player, playing only blues, and give him a quarter to play all those pretty chords they used to go through."[3] I have scores of letters and interviews that attest to the voraciousness of Pops's commitment to his art, ranging from discussions of harmony with pianists to informal seminars on classical technical concepts of double-bass playing.

One of the most fascinating pieces of evidence of Pops's far-reaching musical imagination was related to me by two of the most distinguished traditional jazz bassists in New York City, Bob Haggart and Jack Lesberg.[4]

> At that time (ca. 1958) he was planning a recording with four basses …he was anxious to be part of this quartet idea. I believe he mentioned Milt Hinton, George Duvivier, and myself (since I was present) and why I didn't write something for the sessions (which never materialized).[5]

Needless to say, the idea of a double-bass quartet (in any genre) was visionary at that time. Gunther Schuller wrote what is probably

---

2. Letter from Richard Hadlock to Bertram Turetzky, July 16, 1970.

3. See p. 106.

4. In a July 4, 1970 letter, Jack Lesberg said: "Pops was constantly after me to organize a group of four basses to get something of interest going; unfortunately, this never materialized, but we did get to play together frequently, along with many other well-known bass players such as Bob Haggart, Sid Weiss, Eddie Safranski, etc."

5. Letter from Bob Haggart to Turetzky, July 1, 1970.

the most significant quartet for four basses in 1947, and this piece had to wait until 1957 for its New York City premiere. It is simply incredible to think that one of the original New Orleans jazzmen, age 66; Fred Zimmerman, the "dean of American bass playing," who commissioned the Schuller quartet; and Gunther Schuller, one of America's most important young composers, were thinking along the same wavelength.

The more I did research for this chapter, the more I realized the magnitude of the musical thinking and doing of Foster, and so I decided to let the autobiography tell the story and to concentrate on aspects of his playing style and conclude with discussion of his influence and some critiques.

A study of a large number of photographs, letters, descriptions, and discussions of his playing clearly shows that Pops had what his friend Jack Lesberg termed a "most original technique."[6] His left hand technique was not of the "German school," which still is the main fingering system used in American jazz and symphonic double-bass playing, but something close to what the English refer to as the "fisticuffs" technique. Let us explain the differences with commentary on three characteristic photographs of Pops at work and one of this writer [pages xxv–xxviii]. To begin with, in the classical technique the bass is not held upright, but angled or leaned toward the player in order to get the left hand around the complete fingerboard with ease.[7] Pops held it upright and therefore lost some of the physical ease and power that occurs when the elbow and left hand are almost level with the shoulder. The lowered elbow simply gets in the way; the reader can experience this by trying to emulate Pops.

In all the photographs of Foster, one will notice that his thumb is visible on the left side of the neck like that of a violinist or country guitarist.[8] The thumb traditionally is set behind the second finger[9] in the middle of the fingerboard and acts as a fulcrum, pivot, and guide. The

6. Letter from Lesberg to Turetzky, July 4, 1970.

7. This is a simplification of the standing position and the reader is directed to any of the standard methods of double bass which have photos showing the positions, the bow, and how to hold the instrument.

Figure 1

fingers are arched[10] and the first, second, and fourth (the third is a pressure aid paired with the fourth finger) are employed to produce a half-step each. The "fisticuffs" position necessitates an enormous amount of movement, whereas the "German school" position eliminates much shifting, as the player keeps his hand in proper "shape" and moves only from string to string. For example, in the one-half position,[11] the following pitches are "under the fingers" (Figure 1), and the only movement necessary is to change the arc of the arm to move across the strings, whereas the other method resembles the "hunt and peck" typewriter technique (although it can and does produce artistic results).

Pops, however, grasped one of the most significant elements of left-hand technique, which is the necessity of depressing the string

---

8. *This substantiates Pops's statement that his violinist brother Willie "taught me more about playing the bass than anyone" (See p. 98). Therefore, the often-quoted notion that sister Elizabeth Foster, a cellist, taught him bass should be dismissed on the basis of Pops's words and his use of the thumb. The cellist's thumb is also in the middle of the fingerboard and not at all visible from the front.*

9. *String finger numbering does not count the thumb.*

10. *This is not an academic point, but a question of a most centered sound and greater projection.*

11. *So called because it commences a one-half step from the open string.*

against the fingerboard with enough weight to get the fundamental overtone to dominate the sound. This gives the tone a center (low frequencies need to be perceived carefully) and greater projection. Another important aspect of this concept in left-hand technique is its relation to the "attack and decay" pattern. The securely depressed string produces everything mentioned above plus a long decay time. The jazz bassist today has a prodigious technique that permits him to produce pizzicato (that is, plucked) notes that "ring" and sustain so long that the string community is looking and listening to the double bassists as the leaders in the realm of pizzicato playing.

Pops Foster was one of the few contemporaries who were into this aspect of bass technique, and it should be clear that the aforementioned results of his technique not only made Pops indispensable, but helped the double bass push aside the tuba as the preferred bass instrument in jazz. Gunther Schuller[12] is the first to discuss the attack and decay characteristics of the pizzicato bass in print, but he only mentions the right hand, which is not nearly as important. He does also mention the lowering of the bridge, which helps the left-hand pressure. In conclusion, Schuller articulates the most musicianly discussion of the superiority of the double bass of the tuba I have ever read.[13] This book is hardly the place for a rehash of that tired old argument; besides time has given us the answer.

There is no question that this aspect of Foster's left-hand technique had a great deal to do with one of the most significant components of his style—his powerful sound. "The greatest of these bass players [Al Morgan, John Lindsay, Wellman Braud, and Bill Johnson] is probably Pops Foster, for the extraordinary power of his playing, and his attack, are a precious stimulant to the musicians with whom he is playing."[14] Scores of others wrote and spoke about Pops's drive and power that inspired so many soloists and bands. But it was more than the big sound and the enthusiasm that mattered. There was also his extraordinary innate sense of time. "Pops's rhythm was so sure and

---

12. Gunther Schuller, Early Jazz (New York: Oxford University Press, 1968).

13. Ibid., pp. 159–160.

14. H. Panassié, The Real Jazz (New York: Smith and Durrell, 1943).

firm, San Francisco jazz pianist Vince Guaraldi once said, that he was really better to work with than most young, technically advanced, bassists."[15]

Let us begin a discussion of right-hand techniques with the three basic sound generators: arco (like bowing), pizzicato (i.e., plucking with the fingers), and slapping. Thus there are in reality three different timbres in contrast to the usual one "big sound" pizzicato (and the occasional bowed solo). Slapping is the least familiar of these techniques and is executed in two different ways: the first consisting of slapping the fingerboard with the open palm of the right hand while grasping the finger to be plucked, and the second requiring the string to be pulled up away from the fingerboard. Its subsequent release causes the string to hit the fingerboard and produce the forceful slap (or snap) sound. It is important to note that "slapping" was considered a "hot" sound, like growling through a trumpet or trombone, which affected a timbral transformation as the string bass was converted into a formidable percussion instrument. Slapping was an integral part of Pops's playing throughout his life. In the 1950s and 1960s he slapped less, but we will never know if this was a bow to the ever-changing aesthetic or purely a physical situation. We can, however, authoritatively credit Pops for popularizing this technique. Tony Parenti, who first met Pops in 1918, wrote: "Pops was one of the first original New Orleans bass players that made the slapping bass popular in New York City."[16]

Bowing was an important aspect of the Foster style. "I first learned to bow the bass, then started doing a lot of picking.... It seems like I've been switching like that all my life."[17] He frequently began a piece arco and then changed to pizzicato, thus adding to the rhythmic crescendo that has traditionally been an important element in jazz. Pops used what resembles the "French grip" and utilized both French and German bows. The bow moved from the arm and not the wrist (as is traditionally taught), but it cut the string at the proper angle, and as

15. *Letter from Hadlock.*
16. *Letter from Tony Parenti to Turetzky, July 11, 1970.*
17. *See p. 92.*

he rarely played fast or exposed passages, it did not matter. The arco sound was not *bel canto*, but big and gutty. Technically he was the equal of any recorded jazz bassist before Jimmy Blanton.[18] He could also sing a part in a vocal trio and bow the bass part at the same time...he did that day [in September 1963] as a member of the Hines group."[19] Jack Lesberg says: "I doubt if he had any classical training, however, he did practice and figured out things for himself, as many famous and accomplished players have done."[20] Bill Crow, a veteran New York City bassist, recalls overhearing Foster holding forth on his harmonic approach at Jimmy Ryan's around 1946 or 1947, and he wrote of hearing Pops's voice, dripping with disdain, saying, "Hell, I just play any old go-to-hell note, as long as it swings!" Wrote Crow:

> To me, just beginning to hit what I considered the right notes with anything better than ordinary luck, this seemed sheer old-folks bravado in the face of the wondrous new harmonic intricacies of bop, and may even have been just that. Now, however, after 20 years of learning appropriate bass lines for the changing fashions of jazz and having found three or four musicians, like Jim Hall and Hank Jones, who will take any go-to-hell note one might play and make it sound like a brilliant and gorgeous choice by surrounding it with a heavenly chord, I am inclined to agree with Pops. If the notes you play add to the feeling of swinging together with the rest of the group, then they're probably the right ones.[21]

---

18. *Regarding Blanton, Pops said: "A couple of guys were better at playing melody than me, Jimmy Blanton and Junior Raglin. They could both play a whole lot of melody but had trouble keeping a rhythm foundation. Ragland was a guitar player and Blanton a cello player before they switched to bass. Blanton played string bass like he played the cello" (p. 173). This is one of the two moments of braggadocio to be found in the autobiography.*

19. *Letter from Howard Rumsey to Turetzky, July 16, 1970. Former Stan Kenton bassist Rumsey is best known as the proprietor of the Lighthouse jazz club in Hermosa Beach, California.*

20. *Letter from Lesberg to Turetzky, July 25, 1970.*

21. *Letter from Bill Crow to Turetzky, July 31, 1970.*

This interpretation of Pops's harmonic concepts would have pleased him, I am sure, and it is the most authoritative, articulate discussion of the nitty-gritty of the harmonic responsibilities of the jazz double bassist I have ever read.

Many writers have advanced what Rudi Blesh calls "the base canard that New Orleans jazz is a hippety-hop "two-beat" music."[22] The New Orleans rhythm-section style of about 1920 was quite different and the concept of two-beat bass playing was only one aspect of what was a most sophisticated rhythmic style. In fact, after the 1920s, I feel, a great deal of variety—rhythmic, coloristic, and textural—had been given up to "pump out" the beat. Gunther Schuller refers to the rhythmic variety in discussing John Lindsay's performance in the 1926 Victor recordings of Jelly Roll Morton.[23] Pops tells us: "In New Orleans we'd have two pick [pluck] notes in one bar, then you'd go to six bars of bowing, and maybe have one note to pick."[24] Notes Rudi Blesh:

> Pops often did more than simply "run changes"…frequently (especially if the tune or the chords inspired him) he would build countermelodies to what one or another of the horns was doing. There are not many examples of this, unfortunately, on record, but I have seen him do so many times.
>
> On some such occasions, his bass countermelodies would be projected pizzicato, but frequently—especially in the blues—they would be arco. One good recorded example is to be found in the bowed countermelodies he extemporized with Dan Burley's barrelhouse piano on the Old Circle "skiffle" record, "Dusty Bottom," from the 1946 album *South Side Shake.*
>
> "Dusty Bottom" is a blues slowly and thoughtfully projected by piano with antiphonal bass responses. It is as pure as any Baroque duo—purer, I should say, and Haydn, I'm sure, would have loved it. Edgard Varèse did, anyway. Every time he would visit me he would

---

22. *Letter from Rudi Blesh to Turetzky, August 25, 1970.*

23. *Schuller, Early Jazz, p. 159. Lindsay alternates playing half-notes, whole-notes, and quarter-notes in a most bright and varied manner.*

24. *See p. 92.*

say, "Play that boogie chorale thing!" and I'd get out the old 78 rpm shellac disk.[25]

Also fascinating is Pops's statement from about 1967: "Now we pick four or eight beats to a bar or full note."[26] This and the earlier rhythmic ideas plus the melodic style referred to above are clearly in the avant-garde (that is, those liberated bassists who don't just play time in ensemble.) It would seem that jazz bass playing went around full circle back to this wonderfully rich and varied style that Pops helped promulgate in the early 1900s. One of the main differences between this aspect of the Foster style and the avant-garde is that most of the "new thing" bassists play in the upper registers while Pops played in the lower positions because he felt the bass was a foundation and not a solo instrument.[27] Finally, Charles Mingus, Ray Brown, Richard Davis, Scott LaFaro, and others brought new vistas of velocity of double-bass playing, but let us not forget that fast bassists existed previously. Some of us may remember when Wellman Braud was written up by *Ripley's Believe It or Not* as the world's fastest bass player. This caused another bit of braggadocio as Pops responded, "I know Braud couldn't pick as fast as I could, and I never knew anyone else who could."[28] Whether or not Pops was the fastest is not really important. What we most definitely know is that he was one of the most inspired and inspiring, steady, powerful, and consistently creative bassists in the annals of jazz.

In the 1920s many New Orleans bassists played a two-beat style. Pops was playing a four-beat style, then "when I went to New York playing that way, everybody wanted to do it too. Right after that…about 1929 or 1930…they started writing arrangements that way, with a four-to-the-bar bass part."[29] That "wide" beat and booming, stomping sound dominated many rhythm sections, especially that

---

25. *Letter from Blesh.*

26. *See p. 92.*

27. *See p. 92: "I don't think the bass or the drums are solo instruments; they're the rhythm and I don't like to play solos."*

28. *See p. 173.*

29. *From an unpublished interview with Hadlock, ca. 1964.*

of the famed Luis Russell Orchestra. The Foster sound and approach most definitely led to the bass-dominated rhythm section that jazz history usually tells us that Count Basie, Walter Page, and Jo Jones brought out of Kansas City in the 1930s. It is interesting to note that many of Jones's innovation simply lightened the "drum kit" sound ideal, which made it easier for the powerful Mr. Page[30] to "walk on through," whereas Pops was pitted against some "experimental model" drum sets that really roared. Nevertheless, Pops came through, and it can be said without fear of contradiction that Pops fostered the bass-dominated rhythm section in the 1930s, and this is still the preferred sound in mainstream combo and big band jazz today.

Musicologists have traditionally evaluated performers through documented reports of their prowess from contemporary sources. This time-honored approach will be followed here. Pops had a 70-year playing career; it must be decided when he hit his peak. Many musicians felt that Pops was in peak performance from 1929 on, while others considered the Luis Russell years (1929–1937) the vintage days. How to settle this with scholarly accuracy? I decided to discuss Pops at peak form from 1929 on. Recordings were of some assistance, but, because of the acoustical nature of pre-1950 recordings of the double bass in jazz and the well-known psychological problems of studio recording in general, and in the pretape era in particular, I personally felt that the critique of colleagues would help illuminate many things that are not clear on the recordings, especially for those readers who are not fortunate enough to have heard Pops Foster "rompin' the big fiddle."[31]

> Pops Foster was the greatest of the New Orleans bassists, and perhaps the most flexible. He could swing a big band or trio and anything between. His only peers were Wellman Braud, his contemporary, and the much older Bill Johnson. His beat was an inspiration. What else can I say?
>
> Don Morgenstern, July 14, 1970

---

30. *Page got the nickname "Big Four," but it should be clear now that Pops deserved this appellation earlier than the famous Kansas City bassist.*

31. *"Pops Foster, Forty-eight Years on the String Bass," Jazz Record (March 1947).*

I feel he had a lot for the bass as well as bass players. I always enjoyed him and was amazed when I heard him play…all bass players would go see and hear him. He must have been taking care of business.

Eugene Wright, July 27, 1970

He was always the oldest member of our band [in the 1940s] but the most active and youthful in his playing and personality—when I featured him on the bass, he would always get the biggest hand from the audience.

Tony Parenti, July 11, 1970

I had the pleasure of meeting and hearing the great Pops Foster in the early '30s, with the Luis Russell Band…. He was known by the people who knew all about this kind of music to be the best of his time. He was a great gentleman, very humble, and when I say "humble" I mean in a gracious, dignified way. (Obviously he had not read Harriet Beecher Stowe.)

Bud Freeman, July 10, 1970

Pops was one of the few greats on any instrument one encounters in a musical lifetime.

Art Hodes, August 3, 1970

Most of my recollections of Pops Foster are in the form of indescribable musical sounds which I can hear in my head. (All I do is turn on the mental tape and I can isolate short segments of bass lines heard many years ago at Roseland or on the many great recordings of Armstrong.) This big chomping sound Pops Foster got out of a bass was a driving force and inspiration to me for many years. There was a primitive quality to this sound which appealed to me, and it played a large part in my background and influenced my concept of bass playing…. The first bass sound to catch my ear was Pops Foster and it was his approach to bass playing that inspired me to switch to bass [from guitar] and devote a lifetime to this instrument.

Bob Haggart, July 1, 1970

xxiv The Autobiography of Pops Foster

I don't suppose Pops Foster, technically, could compare with the present generation of bass players, with its symphony refugees and Juilliard graduates. This is not to put them down, but without him, they might still be lost in the symphony forests, hoping, each one, to be the second "serious" player—after the late lamented Serge Koussevitsky—to get a solo spot. Pops Foster may not have done 180 miles per hour on the superhighway. He just laid out the highway, that's all.

Rudi Blesh, August 25, 1970

Educator, author, and composer Bertram Turetzky has advanced the cause of contrabass through his pioneering solo technique, his compositions, his many recordings, and the many solo works written for him.

Bertram Turetzky in the classical playing position.

Pops Foster in his typical arco playing position.

Pops plucking onstage with a single mic picking up his sound.

Classic Pops: Strong grip and a big smile.

Chapter 1
On the Plantation

"This book is gonna straighten a lot of things out."

If I had to do it all over again, I'd do just the same thing I did. But I'd want it like it was when I was a young man around New Orleans. That was kicks. Musicians had fun then and never had any Jim Crow [racial segregation]. Sometimes in my life I've had it good and sometimes bad. One time I had to pawn my bass for six dollars and then had to rent one for a long time because I couldn't scrape up the money to get it out. So it gets rough.

I've always wanted to write down what I know about the times in New Orleans. Some of the books are fouled up on it, and some of the guys weren't telling the truth. One of them says Louis Armstrong played the District. Louis played Saturday nights at Buddy Bartlett's tonk and didn't have no regular job. Guys like Joe Oliver and Freddie Keppard had regular jobs, but most guys around New Orleans didn't. The critics and guys who write about jazz think they know more about what went on in New Orleans than the guys that were there. We had a whole lot of trumpet players around New Orleans besides Oliver and Armstrong. This book is gonna straighten a lot of things out.

The guys that teach music, they're another bunch; they don't know about it. Any of them that see you playing a string bass want to show you how to hold the bow or tell you you aren't fingering right. The teachers always want to tell you to finger the strings with the tip

1

ends of your fingers. You can't finger for tin-can music like that—it's too delicate. You've got to grip those babies to get a tone. All your tone is in the left hand. If you just half muffle the string you don't get no tone; it's like playing with a mute on a horn. It's the same way with the bow. No guy can teach you how to hold it, but all the teachers try. You can't teach people to hold a pencil the way you hold it. You've got to pick it up the way that's most comfortable for you and it's gonna stay that way. All the guys I've taught, I told to hold the bow the way it's comfortable and go on and play.

Some of those critics and dicty [high-falutin'] teachers should see the first bass I had. My brother Willie did most of the work to make it. He put a two-by-four through the hollow of a flour barrel and nailed it on. We used some kinda wood for a bridge and carved some tuning pegs to stick in the two-by-four. Down on the two-by-four we pounded some nails in to tie the strings to. We couldn't afford regular strings so we used twine. It had three strings: We'd twist three pieces of twine together for the lowest, then two, then one for the highest. For two or three days we'd rub the twine with wax and rosin before we'd put them on the bass. The first bow was a bent stick with sewing machine thread tied on it. After a while we got a regular bow without any hair in it. For hair we caught a neighbor's horse and cut the hair off his tail, but it didn't work, and we went back to sewing machine thread. My daddy made us use the bow on it, no plucking. I got awfully sick of sawing on it. We just played it around the house.

My older brother Willie was the first one to take up music in the family. He learned how to play the homemade bass, and then our uncle Wyatt on my father's side hired him to play cello in his little band. Uncle Wyatt was what we called a hamfat violin player—he wasn't so good and he wasn't so bad. Uncle Wyatt would get jobs playing dances around the McCall Plantation from eight at night until four in the morning, and Willie would play for him. Back in those days the band owned the instruments. They'd all put in to buy them, and when you left the band you couldn't take the instrument. If the whole band broke up, whoever ended up with all the instruments could sell them. One day Uncle Wyatt gave Willie a mandolin to play and I got the homemade bass. I've been playing ever since. The earliest I can remember playing, I was seven years old. After a while I started playing in Uncle Wyatt's band too.

Later on Uncle Wyatt sold a cello to my mother for $1.50, and I got to have it for my own. The first real bass I had was a cello. Even after that we didn't have real strings and had to use twine rubbed with wax and rosin. Willie is the one who taught me to play the bass. Willie first learned cello bass, and then he was so fast he learned violin and mandolin too. Later on he picked up banjo, guitar, and all the other stringed instruments.

It wasn't too long after that that Willie, my sister Elizabeth who learned to play guitar, violin, and bass, and I started getting jobs for our little trio playing lawn parties and birthdays in the afternoons and evenings. It seems like we played a birthday every Sunday. I was so small at the time I had to stand on a box to reach the neck of the cello. My brother and sister were both better reading musicians than me, but I could play better and couldn't read so good.

My daddy saw that we had a good thing started, so he got Willie and me to start our own band to put on dances. We called the band the Fosters. None of the field hands around McCall Plantation played anything, but there were a few guys around who played. In our little band we hired a guy named Louie Budour to play valve trombone, and a guitar player. Willie played the mandolin and I played cello or bass. Elizabeth didn't play night jobs with us. Our first guitar player was a guy named Frank who came from around Fort Barrow, Louisiana. He worked on a dredge in the Mississippi River and he was a sleepwalker. One night he walked off the barge and they never found him. Our next guitar player was June Skinner, who worked around the plantation. He played mandolin too.

My daddy would throw the dances on Saturday night. He'd rent an empty house. It would cost 15 cents to get in, and he sold beer. Anywhere from 15 to 20 people would come to them. We'd play quadrilles, polkas, rags, and lancers [sets of quadrilles]. Our little band was very good, and we started taking Uncle Wyatt's jobs away from him. Uncle

Wyatt would have a dance at Richard McCall's plantation and we'd
have one at Harry McCall's. We'd get most of the people at our dance
and he'd get real salty. He started coming around telling my daddy that
he was ruining us kids by keeping us up late playing dances. He carried on about how it wasn't good for us kids. My daddy and him had a
big fight. My daddy told him it was okay as long as he was keeping us
kids up, but when my daddy started doing it, it was bad.

Back in the early days, after we moved to New Orleans, we
needed money pretty bad, so I sold the cello I got at McCall for $1.50
to a little white kid. Later on I tried to get it back, but he wouldn't sell
it. I played the cello in my brother's band for a while before I sold it.

⁂

My daddy, Charley Foster, was no good. He worked for the McCalls
as the butler and spoke French. Everybody who worked in the house
or the yard had to speak French all the time because they wanted
their kids to learn it. I don't think he ever drew any money from the
McCalls. They had the plantation store where you could buy anything, even a horse and wagon. It had a bar, drugstore, and grocery.
My daddy put so much whiskey on the tab there he never drew no
money, and I don't remember him ever buying us kids nothin'. He
went to work early in the morning and got off after he'd served supper. The McCalls usually cooked too much food, and he'd bring
home the leftovers to us or we'd go get them. I always said I'd kill my
daddy. I stole his pistol once, and if it wasn't for the coachman, I'd've
killed him then. I wanted to practice with the pistol shooting a can;
it wouldn't shoot because the safety was on. The coachman saw me
and told my mama, and she took the gun away. I told my daddy,
"When I get to be a man, I'm gonna kill you." Our house at McCall
Plantation was about a city block from the big house where all the
house workers lived. It had great big wide wooden planks for the
floor, and boards on the outside. There was a strip of wood over the
cracks on the outside and some places on the inside. The roof was
made of shingles and there was no ceiling. You could look up and see
the rafters. Once in a while we'd whitewash the walls inside and the

outside was just boards. There was a big fireplace, a really big one. That's where you did all your cooking and got all your heat. We'd make a stack of bricks on two sides, then put iron bars across the center to cook on. It snowed at McCall in the winter, and at night we'd put a great big log in the fireplace to burn all night.

There were two huge rooms in the house. Most of the cooking was done in our room where we had two big beds. Mama had a stove, but most people didn't—they had big pots with legs on them. You baked your bread in a round oven with legs on it, and you put fires on top and bottom. My brother and sister slept in one bed in the big room. I slept in the other, except when my grandmother Martha Foster stayed with us. She slept in my bed. The reason I slept alone was I was always fighting. I'd even hide rocks in my bed so I could throw them at my brother and sister after we went to bed. When my daddy would stay out all night—he didn't hardly stay home at all—my sister slept with my mother.

In the yard outside the house we kept chickens and washed clothes. Back then you washed clothes in a big iron boiler that had a fire under it. You made your soap from ashes from the fireplace and lye. It was the strongest soap you ever wanna see. Out in the yard we kept chickens.

On my mother's side everybody was musical. My grandmother's name was Charlotte Williams. Her people were all from around Donaldsonville, Louisiana. There were a lot of Indians around there, and my mother was nearly full-blooded Cherokee. My cousin Clairborne Williams had a band around Donaldsonville and Plaquemine, Louisiana. Everybody in it was named Williams or related to them, and it was called the Williams Band. Lucy Williams played piano, Clairborne's youngest son played clarinet, his son-in-law played drums—he was the only one not named Williams. Clairborne played trumpet and clarinet, and his brother Michael played bass. They played mostly ragtime music. It's through my mother I'm related to that horse thief Clarence Williams, but I found out about that way late.

My mama, Annie Foster, was 108 years old when she died in 1959. Her mother lived to be over a hundred and had 21 children; Mama was the youngest. She was always knitting, crocheting, and sewing for other people to earn extra money for us. She spoke seven languages—French, Spanish, Latin, Italian, English, and God knows what else. I only speak one and don't do it any good. I remember Mama sewing up a lot of gingham dresses around the plantation. Gingham was the same as silk to the women in those days. Years later on the road the guys used to say, "Don't give me no evening dress, give me a gingham gown, they don't want so much." I knew what they were talking about.

Martin Luther King's funeral reminded me of the funerals on the plantation. They used to put the casket on a long wagon drawn by four mules owned by the plantation. The family and close friends would sit in chairs on the funeral wagon. Then they'd have more mules pulling sugarcane carts with the rest of the people riding on them. It was all very quiet with no music; music was sinful back then.

There were two McCall plantations, Richard's and Harry's, and they were first cousins. I was born on Harry McCall's plantation on May 19, 1892. The ground around the plantation was black bottomland, and there were at least a couple of thousand acres on the place. Some of the people would eat the black mud. They said they liked it; it's salty. There were three or four hundred shacks where the field hands lived about a mile from the house. They all kept chickens, hogs, and cows, and the horses and mules were kept out there. The field hands didn't play any music, not even guitars and sing blues. Up around Fort Barrow there were a lot of guys who played blues on guitar. All of them were colored; you never saw a white man with a guitar or a mandolin.

Around the plantation there were all kinds of trees. There were a lot of sycamores, a few big magnolia trees with beautiful blossoms in the summertime, and some bay trees. Around the big house there was a fence, and inside there were all kinds of fruit and nut trees. One big tree we called a muskeydyne was like a big cherry tree. They had bitter-orange trees, big black fig trees, and pecan trees. Us kids could ask to go through the gate and get the fruit if we wanted, but we'd climb the fence and steal it. If we got caught, we got a good lickin'. All around the house there was a honeysuckle rose vine that smelled so nice, and the bees would buzz around it all summer.

On most Saturday nights we'd play a dance at Harry or Richard McCall's place. Near the plantations there was a little one-horse town called Philadelphia Point where we'd play sometimes. Another place we'd play was Smoke Bend near Fort Barrow. We played a lot of dances in the bouley where the Cajuns live. That's like the backwoods. They're mostly sharecroppers. Most of the Cajuns were halfbreed people who were so mixed up you didn't know what they were.

For the Cajuns we played mostly country or hillbilly music. It's a lot like Jewish music. They liked their music very fast and they danced to it. Some of the numbers they liked were "Lizard on the Rail," "Red, Oh Red," "Chicken Reel," and "Tiger Rag." They had a guy who called figures for them. First you'd play eight bars of a tune, then stop. Then the announcer would get up and call, "Get your partners." When everybody got their partners, he'd blow a whistle and the band would start playing again. The announcer would call the figures like, "Ladies cross, gents right, promenade" and all that stuff. You'd play three fast numbers then take it down to a waltz, a slow blues, or a schottische. The Cajuns would dance till four in the morning and sometimes just go on all night.

All of us kids went to a Catholic school at Donaldsonville about three miles away. After we'd come home, we'd do our homework and practice music. In those days I was crazy about horses. I just loved anything that had to do with a horse. I guess that's why grandmother Foster bought me one. I didn't want nobody using it but me. My daddy would try to loan the horse to a clerk at the store for whiskey. He'd send Willie out to catch it and I'd hear them talking. I'd go out and start shooting rocks at her with my peashooter to make her run off. Willie would run to catch the horse and I'd run and shoot again. Sometimes they wouldn't catch the horse; other times when they'd catch her, she'd be so tired she was no good; and they'd always be late getting her. One time Willie caught her and I threw a cat on her and she threw Willie off and hurt him pretty bad. I loved horses so much

I really didn't want to start playing music. But after I started playing and all the little girls started coming around, I liked it. When I started playing, I was the youngest thing playing for a long time. Now I can't find anyone who started when I did.

In 1900 Harry McCall's son Mac became a lawyer and moved to New Orleans. He got married and settled for a year, then he sent down for Willie to come and work for him. My mother didn't want him to go, but back in those days you did what the whites said to do. He went to New Orleans, and that broke up our little band for a while. In about 1902 my daddy got so bad at drinking and not taking care of us that my mother wanted to leave. She got us out by telling him she was gonna take us to New Orleans to visit Willie. We were gonna stay and he thought so too, so he wouldn't let Elizabeth go. When we left for New Orleans we left with just what we had on. When we got there, we stayed with Willie at the McCall's, in his little old room. Then Mama got a job cooking for the Wilmans and me and Mama moved over there. I had the job of taking Harry Wilman to school and bringing him home so the other kids wouldn't beat up on him.

It wasn't long after that that my grandmother Martha Foster stole my sister from my daddy and brought her to New Orleans. Willie left the McCalls about then because they were gonna beat him up for not serving supper on his night off. He got plenty of jobs working other people's houses after that.

For some reason the McCalls sold the plantation and moved to New Orleans right after that, and they brought my daddy with them.

Pops was ten years old when he emigrated to New Orleans, hometown
for dozens of famous jazz musicians. Behind him Pops left the life of
a Mississippi bottomland plantation with its sprawling village of
shacks, company store (and bar), and great mansion house. The move
to New Orleans required a journey of some 60 miles, sufficiently long
at that time, actually a leap from the 19th century to the 20th. The
feudal enclave of the McCall Plantation was replaced by a corner of
the most cosmopolitan city in America. At the turn of the century,
when Pops arrived, the population of New Orleans exceeded 300,000
persons. They came from a variety of cultural and ethnic back-
grounds—French, Italian, German, Portuguese, English, African, and
Caribbean.

   In New Orleans music was heard at every conceivable social oc-
casion—at parties, dances, political rallies, store openings, parades,
picnics, outings, and funerals. The custom had been established during the permissive rule of governors appointed by the court of Ver-
sailles. After the Louisiana Purchase, French gaiety, permissiveness,
and love of good times continued. An influx of people from other
countries added new colors, rhythms, and melodies to New Orleans
musical style, which became progressively demotic and varied, less
formalized, more subject to change and experimentation.

   New Orleans was one of the great melting pots of music history.
One heard snatches of melody plucked from the latest tango or
French music hall, from a schottische or landler, from Tannhäuser or
Il Trovatore, from John Philip Sousa or Scott Joplin, from a country
folk song or country blues—everything was grist to the musical mill.
Melody was always in great demand; New Orleans musicians were
not overly concerned with harmonic invention; the forms at hand,
simple ideas from band marches and gospel hymns and ragtime, were
sufficient. The main thing was to tailor the material to the requirements of dancers, and, there, too, variety was great: the upper classes
still danced the quadrille and other stately steps handed down from

their European ancestors; in the lowest tonks couples indulged in the most outlandish and unabashed gyrations; and there was every shade of the terpsichorean art in between. For a boy of ten with music in his blood and something of a head start as a string player, New Orleans was a most exciting city in which to live and grow up.

—Ross Russell

Chapter 2

Early Days in New Orleans

*"I didn't do well in school because
I was too busy playing music."*

⚜

On the plantation you didn't see anything but sugarcane and corn. When I first got to New Orleans, I saw wagons going everywhere delivering coal, selling vegetables, and doing different things. In those days the markets opened at three or four in the morning and stayed open till noon. They sold everything you wanted to eat at the outdoor markets. A lot of guys drove vegetable wagons around selling to people in their homes. The vegetable wagons weren't legal, and they had to have fast horses to get away when the cops chased them. When that happened, you could get all the fruit and vegetables you wanted for free; it would fly all over the street. A lot of kids made money driving the vegetable wagons. One guy got so big he had 12 wagons going.

In the heart of town they had a big dump, and if you lived near it you sure could smell the rotten garbage and stuff. Later on they started carrying the garbage out in the Gulf in big barges. We used to have backyard toilets in those days, and colored guys used to come around and clean them out. They'd put the crap in barrels, roll them out to the aggravatin' wagon, then haul them down to the docks and load them on boats, and they'd carry them off down the river. You could smell those aggravatin' wagons for a long way, and the only thing that would kill the smell was lime. The guys who worked the aggravatin' wagons made more money than any of the other colored, but most guys couldn't take it for more than a week. You could smell those guys coming—they smelled terrible. Those outdoor toilets caused some of the biggest roaches you ever saw. They were big red flying ones, and it really hurt when they bit you. The mosquitoes were terrible too. It was so bad in one place we played, named Howard's Canal, we had to wear nets over our heads. New Orleans in those days was a mess. Very few streets had gravel, and only the ones like Canal Street had cobbles; most were just mud.

On Sunday afternoons I used to go out to Lincoln Park. It was a big amusement park. They had a pavilion where a brass band played in the afternoon and people would dance. There were different kinds of things to do, like a merry-go-round, flying horses, a roulette wheel, throw the hoop, and other stuff. The brass band would play the pavilion from about 4:00 to 5:30 P.M. Then they'd have the hot-air balloon ride. They'd get a big fire going and fill this big balloon up with smoke. Buddy Bottle would climb in the basket and go way up in the sky with it. When it got way high, he'd jump out and land by parachute. The balloon would turn over then and come down. Sometimes it didn't work right, and it would take them two or three days to find the balloon. They also had a woman who went up, but I never knew her name.

   After the balloon ride, they had a stage show in the theater. It was a TOBA-style [Theater Owners Booking Association] show with comedians, jugglers, and all that. John Robichaux's band would play the show, which lasted from about 6:00 P.M. to 8:00 P.M. After the stage show, the people would come in and the brass band would take over onstage to play a dance. It cost 15 cents to get in and I was lucky to have a nickel to take the streetcar home, so I had to sneak in. I'd hide behind a post, then get mixed up in the crowd and move on in. Inside

I'd hide around the stage so I could peep at the band. The cop in the place would catch me sneaking around every Sunday and chase me off. Finally, he asked me what I was looking at. I told him I was watching Mr. Kimball play the string bass. He said, "Why don't you learn to play it?" I said, "That's what I'm trying to do." He said, "Okay, you can stay till 9:00 P.M. after this." So after that I could watch Mr. Henry Kimball play till nine. I always thought Mr. Kimball was a wonderful bass player. Years later I was asked to show him how to play.

After my mama got a job in New Orleans, we lived at 2523 Octavia Street. From there we moved up on Broadway. We lived there a little while and moved to Adams Street. When we lived there my brother started working for the Rites people, and that's when he bought me my first bass. My mother and me got along real good; she was comical and had a funny name for everyone. My sister and I couldn't get along for one minute. My mother never had any restrictions on my brother and me—we could stay out as long as we wanted, but Elizabeth couldn't. I usually came home around 10 or 11 at night. Us kids would spend the evening playing around a corner under the street light until one of the cops came along and chased us off. Then we'd go on home or run and hide in the cemetery where we'd play hide and seek.

My father, my uncle Wyatt, and grandmother Foster lived together in New Orleans. My father used to come around to fuss and fight with Mama. One time when he was there I got up behind him with a baseball bat to hit him, but my brother pushed me down. My father told Mama I'd never be no good. Sometimes I used to go over to see my grandmother and take some money over. He'd be there. I'd tell him, "You ain't never been no good to us, and now I've got to take care of you." He'd say, "I'll smash you." I'd say, "No you won't, you used to do that, but not now." He also used to come around where I was playing and want to talk to my boys. It made me mad. He finally got so sick we had to put him in the hospital. They called his sickness TB of the throat, but I think now it would be cancer of the throat. Papa finally died in 1906 at about 50 years old.

I went to school at New Orleans University on St. Charles Street and Leontine. It cost Mama a dollar a month for both my sister and me, and we had to buy our own books. I didn't do well in school because I was too busy playing music. I used to sleep all day in class so I could play at night. In those days if you could play music they'd let you play and pass you. They even loaned us to other schools like Leland University to play their shows. I left school just when I was turnin' to go into the fifth grade—I got a job with the Munson People in Audubon Place and quit school. I always tell kids to finish their schooling before taking up music professionally. I sure wish I had.

All the kids around New Orleans had a goat and a wagon to ride around in. Kids used to get 50 cents to buy a sickle and a shovel. Then you'd go around getting jobs cutting grass to make a little money. You could buy a goat in those days for about 50 cents, and I bought a gang of them. If I'd buy one for 50 cents and a half hour later someone would offer me 75 cents, he'd have a goat. You made your own wagon for the goat to pull out of lumber scraps and old wheels. There was a guy at Oak and Carleton that made harnesses for the goats that cost you two dollars. It took me a long time to get ahold of two dollars.

After I turned professional, I spent a lot of time at Lake Pontchartrain. Sunday was your big day at the lake. Out at the lakefront and Milneberg there'd be 35 or 40 bands out there. The clubs would all have a picnic and have their own band or hire one. All day you would eat chicken, gumbo, red beans and rice, barbecue, and drink beer and claret wine. The people would dance to the bands or listen to them, swim, go boat riding or walking on the piers. The food was mostly every tub; that means everybody takes what he wants and waits on himself. The musicians had just as much fun as the people you played for.

Mondays at the lakes was for the pimps, hustlers, whores, and musicians. We'd all go out there for picnics and to rest up. At night they had dances in the pavilions out on the piers. One night we were playing at the lake and we had a clarinet player named Leb who ate so much fried fish he nearly choked to death. We had to take him home, and he was sick for a long time. He was from Breakaway, Louisiana, where Sam Morgan's from. Some people lived out at the lake all year long. The only time they had to be scared was in a storm.

When I went out at night around New Orleans it was mostly to hear different bands play. I only saw Buddy Bolden's band play once at Johnson's Park. That's where the rough people went. I knew all the guys in the band and later on played with them. Buddy played very good for the style of stuff he was doing. He played nothing but blues and all that stink music, and he played it very loud. Buddy got to drinking so bad they had to hire two trumpets, and Joe Howard played the other one. Joe played on the riverboats with us way late. Jim Johnson the bass player was a very good friend of mine, and I used to hang out with him all the time. He was an older guy than me. Jim liked working with the Bolden Band and stayed with Bolden till he [Bolden] went crazy. Then he went with Jack Carey's Crescent Band. Jim worked on the boats way late and was the last one of Bolden's band to die, in about 1957. He was touring Texas with Don Alberts's band when he got sick and died there. Brock Mumford was the guitar player. Brock had a barbershop at Cherokee and Ann Streets in the heart of what was called Niggertown. Most of the guys in Bolden's band were barbers. Willie Warner was on clarinet and Frank Lewis played another one. Frank Keeley played valve trombone with the band for a while, then Willie Cornish took over. Willie and I played with Freddie Keppard, and I played other jobs with him at Milneberg and around New Orleans. Willie was a plasterer and bricklayer. None of the band could read. Frankie Dusen never played with the band, but he took it over and named it the Eagle Band after Buddy blew his top. Frankie was one of those cheeky guys. There was another guy around named Buddy Bolden, but he didn't play nothin'.

From about 1902 to about 1906, when I joined the Rozelle Band, I played with little groups and trios for lawn parties and fish fries. All over New Orleans on Saturday night there'd be fish fries. The lawn parties were usually Monday or Wednesday night. If the guys didn't have a job to play a lawn party, they'd put on their own and hire somebody's yard. When you gave a lawn party or a fish fry you had to go to the police station and get a permit to have one that cost 50 cents. Then you had to have a policeman on duty that cost your $2.50 or $3.00. Most of the time you just hired a policeman you knew, then you didn't have to take out no permit. To advertise, you'd get a carriage with the horses all dressed up, a bunch of pretty girls, and then the musicians would get on, and you'd go all over advertising for that night. Down at the Jackson Brewery or whatever one you thought was best, you'd buy kegs of beer. A quarter-keg cost you 80 cents and you got three or four, then packed them down with ice to keep them cold, and sold it for ten cents a glass. The wife usually did the cooking in the morning. She'd fry catfish, cook gumbo, make ham sandwiches, potato salad, and ice cream to sell. The man would get the beer, wine, and whiskey. When it got toward dark, you'd hang a red lantern out on the front door to let anybody going by know there was a fish fry inside and anybody could go in. A plate of catfish and potato salad or a plate of gumbo was 15 cents. It usually cost 25 cents to get in and it was a good way to make a little change.

Around Chicago and New York they had the same thing but they called them "house rent parties." In New York you'd even get invited to a birthday party and they'd charge you to get in. After some of the guys from New Orleans went to Chicago, they started giving fish fries in the bars. At the door you'd buy a ticket and get a lucky number. If you won the drawing you'd get a bottle of whiskey.

The fish fry that had the best band was the one that would have the best crowd. The band was usually a string trio of mandolin, guitar, and bass, and sometimes violin, guitar, and bass. String trios would get a whole lot of jobs around New Orleans where they wanted soft music. Some guys were big stars on the mandolin and would draw a crowd to a fish fry. Buddy Kyle was one of them who played a whole lot of mandolin and was very hard to book. He played a lot of jazz.

Elmer Snowden played banjo like Buddy played mandolin. It was a lot more pleasure for me to play in the string trios than in the brass band.

There were always 25 or 30 bands going around New Orleans. There were all kinds of work for musicians from birthday parties to funerals. Out at the lake they had some bands in the day and others at night; Milneberg was really jumping. There were a lot of string trios around playing street corners, fish fries, lawn parties, and private parties. The piano players like Drag Nasty, Black Pete, Sore Dick, and Tony Jackson were playing the whorehouses. In the district there were the cabarets, Rice's, Fewclothes, Huntz and Nagels, and Billy Phillips who had the best bands. Some bands played dances in milk dairy stables, and the bigger-name ones played the dance halls like the Tuxedo Dance Hall, Masonic Hall, Globes Hall, and the Funky Butt Hall. The bands played picnics out at the lake; they played excursions on the riverboats and for the trains. The restaurants like Galatoires on Dauphine Street had bands. On Chartres Street there was Jackson Square Gardens where they had two or three bands going. There were tonks like Real Tom Anderson's at Rampart and Canal and Tom Anderson's Annex at Iberville and Basin Street. Out in the country, like Breakaway, Louisiana, or Bay St. Louis, Mississippi, you played dances, fairs, picnics, and barbecues. We had plenty of fun together and there was music everywhere. If the rest of the world was like musicians, this would be a great world. You should see musicians backstage when one band comes back to see another. Jesus, there's some noise and talk.

The first band I was with regular was the Rozelle Band. It was started in 1905 by my brother, Roy Palmer, Ovette Jackson, and a guy named Rucker. I started playing with them in 1906, and that's when Willie bought me my first real bass. They were a seven-piece band, and that was a big band. We had some good musicians in the Rozelle Band. Our first guitar player was Ralph Honis. The last time I saw him was in Chicago in 1962; he may still be alive. Ralph gave up guitar and started playing trumpet, so we got another guitar player, Joe Johnson. After that Ralph switched to trombone and Joe switched to trumpet, so we got another guitar player. Joe was a very good guitar player, but my brother had an E-flat trumpet and Joe kept borrowing it. Sam Dutrey taught him how to play it and he switched about 1907. Joe was very good on trumpet and took Joe Oliver's place in Frankie Dusen's Eagle Band later on.

Back in the early days, all of us guys used to hang out at Sam and Nora Dutrey's pressing shop at Cherokee near St. Charles Street. There were four Dutrey brothers: Sam, who played clarinet; Honoré (we called him Nora), who played trombone; Jimmy, who played drums; and Pete the violin player. Sam and Nora always wanted us guys to hang out at their shop, and Sam would give us free music lessons to get us to stay. I never will forget when the Dutrey brothers and me went to Joe Johnson's funeral in about 1914. The preacher sure did lay it on us, but that's later.

The Rozelle Band played a lot of lawn parties and milk dairy stable dances. In those days there were milk dairy stables all over New Orleans. Guys would hire the stable and clean it out for the dances. Most of the time the owner of the stable would put on the dance. They were on Saturday, Sunday, and Wednesday nights. Most milk dairy jobs you'd get 75 cents to $1.25 to play. You'd start playing at 8:00 P.M. and the dance would last until 3:00 A.M. or 4:00 A.M. A lot of parents would come to the dance, bring their kids, and stay all night. In the morning you'd be playing along and outside you'd hear the cows start mooing because they wanted to come in and get milked. When that started you knew the dance was over. Sometime we'd be romping real good and keep playing with the mooing going on. Those times they'd open the doors, bring the cows in, and run us out.

Back in those days I was real small and still had to stand on a box to reach the string bass right. I always told Willie that the string bass was too big for me to carry. I'd carry his violin or banjo on a job, and he'd carry my string bass. Then one time I got a job and had to get there right away. Willie wasn't around so I carried the bass. He wouldn't carry it for me after that.

I remember that a bunch of us young guys heard about the Holiness church back then, where you went down and rolled around with everybody. We thought it meant you could go down there, pick out a chick, and roll around with her. So we went down and they threw us out. The Holiness church was the only one that didn't consider music sinful. Their music was something. They'd clap their hands and bang a tambourine and sing. Sometimes they had a piano player, and he'd really play a whole lot of jazz. You should've heard it. Way late they added things like guitars, trombones, trumpets, and so on. The first time I heard one of their bands was about 1930 in Washington, D.C. We used to hurry to finish our theater job so we could go listen to them play. They really played some great jazz on the hymns they played. My sister, Elizabeth, joined the Holiness church in the late '20s and played guitar for them. She really thought they were somethin'. The closest thing we had to religious music around New Orleans was when the bands played for funerals.

I was with the Rozelle Band for about two years. Around 1908 we moved to St. James Street near St. Thomas Street. The Rozelle Band broke up and we went our separate ways. Down around St. James Street I met Eddie Garland; we always called him Montudie. He was playing with the Ory Band and got me a job playing with a little band that Louis Keppard had. It was called the Magnolia Band, and we got Joe Oliver to play in it after that.

Charley Foster, Pops's father, about 1900.

Charley Foster, Pops's father, about 1900.

Annie Foster, Pops's mother, about 1940.

Willie Foster, Pops's brother, about 1925, New Orleans.

Willie Foster and Henry Kimball, Sr., about 1925, New Orleans.

William Bebe Ridgley, trombonist and leader of the Tuxedo Orchestra.

The Fate Marable Band on the SS Sidney out of New Orleans, about 1918. From left: Baby Dodds, drums; Bebe Ridgley, trombone; Joe Howard, trumpet; Louis Armstrong, trumpet; Fate Marable, piano; Dave Jones, mellophone; Johnny Dodds, clarinet; Johnny St. Cyr, banjo; Pops Foster, bass.

Eddie Allen's Gold Whispering Orchestra playing on the SS Capitol, about 1921. From left: Harry Lankford, trombone; Sidney Desvignes, trumpet; Floyd Casey, drums; Eddie Allen, trumpet; Johnny St. Cry, banjo; Isaac Jefferson, piano; Walter Thomas, saxophone; Pops Foster, tuba and string bass; Norman Mason, saxophone; Gene Cedric, clarinet.

Advertising card for W.C. Handy, about 1910. Handy had just resigned from Mahara's Minstrels and resettled in Memphis as a bandleader and teacher.

W. C HANDY,
Teacher of Band, Orchestra,
AND
Vocal Music.

W.C. Handy in a photo signed to Pops Foster, about 1940. Handy was then head of his own publishing company in New York.

Kid Ory's Band, Los Angeles, 1922. From left: Kid Ory, trombone, Thomas "Papa Mutt" Carey, trumpet; Fred Washington, piano; Bud Scott, banjo; Theodore Bonner, saxophone; Billy Butler, saxophone; Pops Foster, tuba and string bass. Not shown: Leon White, drums.

Advertising card for the Black and Tan Orchestra, Los Angeles, about 1915. From left: Paul Howard, saxophone; Ernest "Nenny" Coycault, trumpet; Leon Herriford, clarinet; James H. Jackson, piano; H.A. Southard, trombone; Leon White, drums.

Curtis Mosby's Dixieland Blue Blowers. The band is playing from a truck-driven float advertising a Charleston contest, presumably August 6, 1923, at Solomon's Penny Dance Hall in downtown Los Angeles. From left: Henry Starr, piano; unknown, slide cornet; Bob Brassfield, saxophone; Freddie Vaughn, banjo; Harry Barker, trumpet; Lloyd "Country" Allen, trombone; Curtis Mosby, drums.

Musicians' get-together, Los Angeles, 1925. From left: Marcellus Levy, drums, Peacock Melody Strutters; Harry Barker, cornet, Lloyd Allen, trombone, Curtis Mosby, drums, Curtis Mosby's Dixieland Blue Blowers; "Meyers," cornet, Sonny Clay's Plantation Orchestra; Willie Porter, cornet, Sunnyland Jazz Band; Alex Levy, reeds, Peacock Melody Strutters.

Eddie "Montudie" Garland,
Oakland, California, about
1928, in the Elks Marching
Band uniform similar to one
worn by Foster in 1927.

Lionel Hampton,
about 1932.

The rise of a professional class of jazz musicians in New Orleans came with the second decade of the century, and the process was a gradual one. In the beginning a man played as an amateur, and by attaching himself to an organized group of older and more experienced musicians, he served a loose apprenticeship and, eventually, if talented and persistent, was taken along on a job and handed a dollar for his services. There was no union in those days. Jobs were booked by individual contractors who were also bandleaders; slowly bands like Magnolia, Tuxedo, and Eagle evolved. For a long time, music remained an avocation, for most every musician had a day trade. He was a barber like Buddy Bolden, a plasterer like Johnny St. Cyr, a tinsmith like Alphonse Picou, a cigar maker like Manuel Perez, or a longshoreman like Pops Foster. Many leading jazzmen worked at hard manual labor; jazz drew some of its best talents from proletarian ranks, and working-class virtues rubbed off in the music. Bolden, Keppard, Armstrong, and Bechet owed their reputations in part to an ability to keep going, to pile chorus upon chorus, creating a feeling of suspense and excitement in the listener. Of course, this demanded instrumental technique and an abundance of musical ideas. It also demanded an uncommon amount of physical endurance. Such demands were imposed to an even greater degree on men in the rhythm section, especially the drummers and bassists. Strength, endurance, and solidity were manifest in Pops's playing from the very first; his beat was compelling and powerful, his tone big and alive.

In speaking of Lorenzo Tio and Alphonse Picou, Pops is referring to leading members of the school of master New Orleans clarinetists who descended from the old Creole class. New Orleans Creoles were of mixed European and African blood; at one time they had formed a petite bourgeoisie class. They spoke French and prided themselves on being co-heirs of French culture. The incidence of musical attainment in Creole ranks was high. All had studied with French teachers and a few aspired to jobs in the pit bands of the French theater and

opera. As colonial Frenchmen, they were one with the tradition of distinguished French reed playing. In the free and easy atmosphere of
prebellum New Orleans, Creoles were considered every bit as good as
white folk. The Civil War and the violent upheavals of postbellum
days changed all that; the Creoles were cast down as a class, stigma-
tized by their fractional content of African blood. The musicians
among them found themselves obliged to compete for jobs with the
black man. Socially the clash between déclassé and parvenu made for
a certain amount of hostility and bitterness. Musically it was benign;
the emerging New Orleans style, already enriched by elements from
so many diverse musical cultures, further benefited from the marriage
of the two schools: the clean, pure, limpid playing of the Creoles and
the rough, more dynamic style of the African Americans.

"The District," as Pops points out, was a wartime casualty. It was
also called Storyville, after a New Orleans alderman, much to that
gentleman's dismay; Sidney Story had been the author of an ordi-
nance restricting prostitution, gambling, and other forms of vice to a
specified area in the French Quarter (1897). Tom Anderson, proprietor of Anderson's Annex where Pops worked, was the ward's political boss and city councilman as well as the owner of other cabarets,
real estate, and shares in several of the most popular bagnios in "the
District," which enjoyed the reputation of being the most extensive
area in America devoted to vice. According to social historian Herbert
Asbury (The French Quarter), in 1910 the official count of houses of
ill repute was 175 and the total number of registered prostitutes in ex-
cess of 800. Of these 700 were full-time employees of houses of prostitution, which ranged from lowly cribs to the famous and resplendent
Mahogany Hall on North Basin Street, operated by Lulu White.
About 100 part-time ladies of the night worked in cabarets, where
they danced with customers, encouraged the purchase of liquor—
especially champagne—and escorted interested customers to nearby
rooms for amorous asides, all as described by Pops. Knifings and fights
were common and murders frequent. The District swarmed with
hoodlums, burglar gangs, and the Mafia, then known as the Black
Hand. The pressures that resulted in the shuttering of Storyville orig-
inated in Washington and came shortly after America entered World

War I. When the official suggestion was not acted upon by local authorities, the latter was put on notice that either they would close Storyville without delay or the federal government would do it for them; New Orleans had become the favorite duty station for tens of thousands of servicemen. The actual closing date was November 12, 1917.

The candid Pops Foster makes no effort to play down the licentious environment encountered and something relished by early jazz musicians. This association of jazz with vice hung on in the minds of most Americans for years and died hard; the notion fitted perfectly into widespread prejudice encouraged by the middle-class white establishment toward African-American mores and culture.

The essential point is that musicians, like other professional workers, depended upon jobs for a livelihood. From about 1900 to 1917, the best paying and steadiest employment for jazzmen was to be found in Storyville. It was not until the middle '30s with their swing bands and popular ballrooms that conditions of employment for jazz musicians underwent any significant change.

When Pops began working in Storyville, he was a young man of 16 or 17. Magnolia was one of the leading bands of that time. Joe (later King) Oliver was just then attaining the peak of his powers. Oliver, Freddie Keppard, and Bunk Johnson belonged to the second generation of New Orleans trumpet players who followed Buddy Bolden.

—Ross Russell

Chapter 3

The Magnolia Band in the District

"Most of us loved the District....
Sometimes I didn't go home for weeks."

❧

Music was a nice sideline to make a little change back in early New Orleans, but I never thought it would be a way to make a living. I usually had a regular job longshoring or something. My job with the Magnolia Band in the District was the first music job that was a full-time job.

When I first started with the Magnolia Band, we made most of our money on Saturday, Sunday, and Wednesday. Sunday was the biggest day, and we made a little money on Monday. I used to do longshore work, drive a cotton wagon or coal wagon, and a lot of other things besides play in the band. It was pretty rough playing and working a full job too; Monday was your roughest day. On Sunday you might have an afternoon job at the lake playing a picnic till six o'clock. Then you'd get on a streetcar and go way over to Gretna to play a night job at the Come Clean Hall. Back in those days when you took the string bass on the streetcar you had to have a special pass. Over in Gretna we used to play the Big Easy Hall and the Drag Nasty Hall. (It's still in Gretna.) The Primrose Band that was led by Hamp Benson had the Sunday job at the Come Clean

Hall until we came along and took it away from them. We had a rough band. Hamp was a trombone player, and Joe Johnson played trumpet with them. They were guys from around the Irish Channel.

You might play a dance from eight that night till four o'clock the next morning. You'd go home then, hang up your tuxedo, put on your overalls, and leave about 5:00 A.M. and catch the streetcar to the stables. There you'd pick up your mule team at 6:00 A.M. and start out for the docks to pick up a load at 7:00 A.M. Once you got your team hooked up and started toward the docks, you could sleep because your mules would follow the wagon in front. Sometimes you had a helper; he'd drive the wagon where you were going and you'd sleep. He'd wake you up to load or deliver. You got off work about four o'clock in the afternoon. If you had a Monday-night job you'd go home, get a little shuteye, and start playing at eight o'clock. You didn't work late on Monday night, though. After I started doing longshore work, it wasn't so rough. I'd work a couple of hours, then put somebody in my place and go on home.

When I joined the Magnolia Band in early 1908, Louis Keppard, Freddie's brother, was the leader and manager. He played guitar. They had a job playing a house party and hired me for it. They were crazy about my playing so they kept me with them. Johnny Garland was on trombone when I first started with them, but he wasn't so good so we got rid of him and got Zue Robertson for a while. Zue could play all styles real good. He was one of the best players around. Zue could play piano very good too, but he never played it with the band. He played piano before the trombone. He wasn't with us too long, and he left to go on the road with his sister and brother-in-law in a vaudeville show. They had a comedy act named McNeil and McNeil, and Zue played piano for them. After Zue left we had Eddie Atkins on trombone and sometimes Honoré Dutrey.

Harrison Goughe was our first trumpet player. He couldn't play unless he looked at the music, and he stunk. We got Joe Oliver to come with us about the middle of 1908 when he quit the Eagle Band. Arnold Dupas played drums and Dave Dupas played clarinet for us.

Emile Bigard played violin; he was Barney Bigard's uncle. The Dupas brothers and Emil were close friends. After I was with the band for a while, the guys wanted to get rid of Arnold Dupas because he wasn't any good on drums. They were afraid that if they fired Arnold that Dave and Emile would quit. So they fired all three of them. When you got fired in those days they'd shove a letter under your door. All it said was, "You are fired." We got Jean Vigne on drums after that, but he slept so much so we fired him and got a guy named Chris. After we went into the District, we had Ernest Trippania; we called him Quank. My brother Willie replaced Emile on violin. Alphonse Picou played clarinet for us sometimes, and sometime Papa Tio did. Picou was the only guy around who played soprano saxophone. Most guys said it sounded too tinny. Papa Tio said to Picou one time, "Where're you taking that tin clarinet?" Picou got mad, and they didn't speak for years over it. A soprano is very hard to tune and to play in tune. Some of the notes are beautiful and some are out of tune. Years later Sidney Bechet and I used to argue about that all the time.

Papa Lorenzo Tio was a nice old guy. He was tall and drank a lot. One night he was playing for the Magnolia Band. He was drunk and sleeping through the numbers. He'd get the clarinet up to his mouth and finger the horn, but nothin' was coming out. I got a broomstick, picked up his clarinet, and put the broomstick on his lap. He played the whole next number on the broomstick. When Joe Oliver got ready to knock off for the next number he asked Tio, "Tea, you gonna play this next number with us?" Tio said, "I've been playing all night, man. Don't you like my playing?" Joe said, "What are you playing with?" He said, "My clarinet," and took a look at it. Then he turned to me and said, "You did this."

Joe Oliver joined the Magnolia Band about the middle of 1908. Before that he waited tables at private parties and played with Frankie Dusen's

Eagle Band on Saturday night. He met his wife, Stella, when they were
working together waiting tables. Joe got mad one night and quit the
Eagle Band, and came with us. I never heard anybody down there
called "King." If Joe Oliver and Louis Armstrong were called "King"
around New Orleans, I never heard any of it. Joe got to cutting everybody around Chicago with his horn, and that's where they started calling him "King."

Right after Joe joined us we got the job playing in the District.
When we started I was so young, I had to be careful of the cops running me in just for being there. They didn't allow no kids in the District at night. There were two cops on every corner in the District.
When I'd go to work I'd be careful to stay on the side of the street
where I knew the cops. Once I got to work, I stayed inside. The girls
inside would be sitting with their dresses up to their knees, and I'd get
to see a lot of legs. That was something in those days. Before that us
kids used to go downtown just to watch the girls pull up their dresses
to get on the streetcars. We used to be happy when it rained because
we could see more. Things were right on top of each other in the District. Freddie Keppard was at Billy Phillips's on one corner. Manuel
Perez was on the same corner at Rice's. Our band was on the next corner at Huntz and Nagels at Custom House and Liberty. They were
two Jew guys and were good guys to work for. In the middle of the
block was the Tuxedo Dance Hall. It was owned by Gyp the Blood.
He went to the penitentiary after he killed Billy Phillips and his place
closed. All the guys who played at the Tuxedo Dance Hall wore tuxe-
dos, and that's where they got the name for the band. Even after the
killing and both places closed down, the band kept the Tuxedo name.
When all of us were playing the District, we couldn't wait for night to
come so we could go to work. Most of us loved the District and tried
to stay there as much as we could. Sometimes I didn't go home for
weeks.

We made a dollar and a half a night, or nine dollars a week playing the District. We were the best-paid band in the District. You could
live real good on it and save money. We hired a guy for a dollar a night
to pass the hat around for us. If a good German ship came in, we'd
make ten or 12 dollars apiece in tips. Those guys would give you all

their money. The German guys would drink wine and champagne and have a good time. The Dutch and English sailors were kind of rough. They'd drink beer; we had Budweiser or Schlitz in those days, and it was as strong as your whiskey is today. They didn't spend much money until they got real drunk. The French were nowhere. We had some beautiful girls in our cabaret, and if a good ship came in we'd pass the word for all the girls to get out that night. A lot of the girls were white. In those days carpenters and bricklayers made 13 dollars a week, and guys who dug ditches and things like that made a dollar and a half a day. I thought we had it easy sitting up on that stand playing music all night. If you were just working on night jobs you usually got a dollar-fifty a night. On Easter Sunday and if you got a job playing one of those swell dances downtown you made two-fifty.

Long after I left New Orleans guys would come around asking me about Storyville down there. I thought it was some kind of little town we played around there that I couldn't remember. When I found out they were talking about the red-light district, I sure was surprised. We always called it the District.

Liquor at the cabarets was high. They had two kinds of whiskey. Best whiskey was I.W. Harper, Murrayhill, and Sunnybrook that cost ten cents in the tonks and 20 cents in the cabarets. Second-best whiskey came in a barrel and was five cents in the tonks and ten cents in the cabarets. Everything in the cabarets was about double the regular price. You used to get half of a big soda pop bottle full of whiskey for a nickel. There was only one kind of champagne, and it came in a little bottle or a big bottle. You had white wine and sherry wine, and the Italians had a drink they called Angaliquor. You could get a big cup of it for ten cents. The guy wouldn't even watch you take it because he knew you couldn't drink more than a dime's worth. It tasted something like sherry wine. I think it was leftovers from all the other wines, and they only sold it in the Italian barrelhouse joints. Sometimes a good party didn't come in the cabarets until 3:30 or 4:00 in the morning. We'd have our instruments half packed getting ready to go. We'd unpack and start playing. As long as they stayed, we'd play. Sometimes it lasted until 4:00 the next afternoon. Your normal playing was eight hours, but that didn't mean nothin' if there were customers in the place.

In the District none of the dance halls and cabarets served food, just booze except when Carrie Nation would come around. She was always coming around with three or four guys to check you out. She expected food to be served and all the girls to be standing on the dance floor. If she was around checking the District, the places would call each other to let you know she was headed in your direction. The owner would get some sandwiches out on the bar and the girls on the floor. If she caught you without food or with a girl sitting down drinking whiskey, she'd break up all the whiskey in the place with her ax.

A cabaret in New Orleans had the bar in the front where you walked in. All the girls stood around in the middle of the floor facing the door. The band was way at the back, at the end of the dance floor. When you came in you picked out a girl you wanted to dance with and got some tickets. They cost you 25 cents apiece and were good for one dance. The girl took half your ticket before the dance, then at the end of the evenings they turned them in for ten cents each. The length of the dance was according to the crowd, but you never played a whole number. On a good night you'd play a half of a half chorus. You never started and played the number all the way through, and you never stopped playing for a break. If a guy sat at a table with a girl and bought her champagne, he still had to give her a ticket for a dance. The girls got 25 or 30 cents on every bottle of champagne a customer bought. If you wanted to go off to bed with her, it was 50 cents to a dollar depending on how business was—a dollar was tops. They could take a man out and do their little business, but she had to bring him back to buy some more drinks. If she didn't bring him back, she didn't come back. There were dance-hall girls in a lot of places. The big places like Huntz and Nagel's, Eddie Groshey's, Gyp the Blood's, and Billy Phillips's had big seven-piece bands. The small places had piano, or piano and drums, or maybe another instrument or two.

Besides the dance-hall girls, there were girls who just stuck their heads out of their cribs. There were the big sporting houses like Lulu

White's, and women down around where Louis Armstrong lived that were only ten or 15 cents. They didn't look so good though. On Monday it was your day off in the District, and sometimes you didn't go back to work until Wednesday night. You'd get some of the girls, a picnic lunch, and go out to the lake. Sometimes we'd hire a little band to entertain us, and we'd eat and swim. Everybody got along real good and had good times.

All the musicians back in New Orleans wanted to be pimps. You had a lot of girls who went for you, and you'd put your girls to work on the line. Pimping in those days was a lot of guys' head line, and Jelly Roll Morton was one of them. He only played piano as a sideline because you had to prove you were doing some kind of work or they'd put you in jail. Jelly was very good looking and had some good women. We'll talk about him later—I got some things to say on him. The girls back in those days liked to have a good-looking man they took care of. The girls gave you money, bought you clothes, and sent you out looking nice. If you mistreated your girl or she caught you talking to another girl, she'd get mad and call the cops and send you to jail.

The cops didn't want no man living off a woman; they wanted you to work. If you had more than one girl on the line you had to meet them at different times and be very careful. The cops would raid the District once in a while. They'd search the girls' cribs to see if there was any man's clothes in them. If a raid was coming, the cop on the beat would warn you trouble was coming. He'd just say, "Beware, man!" Sometimes you'd get the word from Henry the bartender at the Twenty-five Club; he'd say, "Pass the word there'll be a raid tomorrow morning." When you lived in the District you only kept some socks, a toothbrush, and razor at your girl's, in a cigar box. When the cops would get raw on the pimps, you'd see all the guys moving out carrying their cigar box.

There were some big-time pimps around the District. Even the guys who worked as musicians would be lining up tricks for their girls. The really big-time hustlers, like Roy Nunez's old man, worked hard at it and made a lot of money. He had a diamond stud as big around as a nickel. Jelly always had two or three girls on the line for him, and that's where he got his diamond tooth. All the pimps wanted to have diamond studs, cuff links, belt buckles, and [diamonds] on their teeth.

Around 1909, when the Magnolia Band was playing the District, we had Big Eye Louis Nelson working with us. Louis had a chick working out of a crib right across the street from us. Where I was standing on the bandstand, I could look out and see her. Every time she'd turn a trick she'd clean herself with some water and throw it out the door. Then she'd come out with a broom and scrub the front with it to draw another trick. Every time she'd scrub, I'd mark it on the wall with a piece of chalk. At 4:00 A.M. when we'd get off, Louis would ask me how she'd done. I'd call the number. Then when we'd all meet at the Twenty-five Club, Louis would ask her how it went. She'd say, "Oh, babe, I didn't do so good, I just had five." He'd say, "You're a damn liar." She wondered for a long time how Louis knew how many tricks she turned. Before we'd go to work at 8:00 P.M., all the guys and girls would gather at the Twenty-five Club starting about seven for some fun and talk before we went to work. Then when we'd get off, we'd all meet again at 4:00 A.M. During the day us guys used to hang out at a pool hall at Dumaine and Claiborne. After a while Henry Ponts started putting all the names of the musicians up on the wall and serving an oyster loaf for 15 cents. So the musicians started to play pool and hang out there.

I had a couple of girls on the line when I was in the District. You're down there with all the pimps and hustlers, and you want to be like them. One girl I had was named Edith. Joe Oliver carried me to her and introduced me. I was only 16 or 17 at the time, and she was way older than me. I was scared to death of her, mostly because Joker Joe was trying to go with her, and I was afraid he'd fire me. When Joe came down to her place one day and found me lying up in her bed, Joe got real hot and was gonna fire me. Eddie Groshey, our boss, told Joe, "Let the boy alone, Joe, Jesus Christ. Go on out and get yourself another gal." After that Joe would tell me every night, "You go out there to see her and get cut, you ain't got no job."

One evening I thought I had been shot down. I was going into a place called Platt's to have an oyster loaf. Just as I got to the door I heard a pistol go off. Then I heard another shot go *zing*. I ran inside and hit my shoulder on the door when I did. When I got inside I knew I was shot in the shoulder, and nobody could tell me I hadn't been hit.

One time Johnny St. Cyr and I were going home one Christmas morning about 3:00 A.M. We met Tom Benton on the street so drunk he couldn't find his way, so we decided to take him home first. In those days if you were drunk out on the street the cops would put you in jail until you sobered up, and if you were with a drunk they threw you in too until he sobered up. The cops got us and we all went to jail. Johnny and I had a date to make and we had to get out. Tom seemed to get drunker, and it looked like he wasn't ever gonna sober up. We ask the jailer to bring us a block of ice. When he did we took that baby and tied it up between Tom's legs. In about two minutes he was sober and they let us out.

All the girls, pimps, and other guys who worked the District and were doing illegal things used to pay a lawyer seven dollars a month to keep them out of jail. I paid him for a while. His name was Lee Peyton. You knew you were gonna get picked up sometime if you were illegal, and he could get you right out. You just called him. You hardly ever went before a judge, and if you did he'd dismiss you.

In the District the guys in the band would get four or five drinks bought for them by some guy at the bar. Some of us would keep a bottle and pour the whiskey in the bottle to save for Christmas. Christmas was a big day then. New Year's Eve was nothin' for parties or dances. Everybody went to church. It was a jinx to have a dance on New Year's Eve. The Mardi Gras day was something, back about 1910. Everybody started getting together about six o'clock in the morning. We'd start fooling around and having a good time. We'd have a big wagon with a five- or six-piece band, a lot of girls sitting around on it, and kegs of beer sitting on the tail of the wagon. The band would play and we'd go around to different peoples' houses. They'd have homemade donuts, hot coffee and tea, whiskey and stuff to drink. Everybody would play and dance for a while, then we'd take off for another house. That would go on all day. The people from New Orleans cut up and had their own fun. The people from out of town went down on Canal Street and saw the parade with about 20 floats and the bands. They didn't have any colored bands playing in the parade. Some of the colored guys played in the bands but they passed for whites. During Lent everything closed down except the saloons where you could get a drink. All the guys had a trade like cigar maker, carpenter, bricklayer, or barber, so they'd go to work for the 40 days of Lent.

People go to the French Quarter now and they think the hot spots we played were along Bourbon Street. Back then Bourbon Street was just a bunch of furniture and jewelry stores. We used to have our gold belt buckles made there.

I played with the Magnolia Band from early 1908 to the middle of 1910. After that I played with them and freelanced around. I was the bass player around there, and whoever had the work, that's who I was with. I was with Buddy Petit, Jack Carey's band, the Silver Leaf Band, and Frankie Dusen's Eagle Band. Later I went on the boats with Fate Marable and worked Tranchina's at Spanish Fort with Picou.

In 1910 after Gyp the Blood killed Billy Phillips, they closed all the cabarets down and we were out of a job for a while. They opened them back up in early 1911 and things were good until the war came along. In 1914 they closed the District down really tight and made all the chicks go to work. I went to work in the iron foundry driving a little spring wagon. I learned all about the foundry, how to melt iron, cast iron and steel. After I learned they gave me a whole gang of women from the District to work for me. I'd have them pickin' out iron for me, and I'd sleep. Closing the District hurt the women a lot more than it did the musicians because they didn't know no other work. Most of the musicians around New Orleans didn't work the District so it didn't hurt them at all. Billy Phillips's and Gyp the Blood's places were already closed from the shooting. Fewclothes's, Rice's, and Huntz and Nagel's cabarets closed, and the Tuxedo Dance Hall. The piano players in the whorehouses were all out of work. Most of the dance halls were out of the District and only opened on Friday, Saturday, Sunday, and Monday nights. None of them closed. They kept going on like before, and that's where most of the bands worked.

A lot of musicians left New Orleans before the District closed. Laurence Duhé was one of the first to leave about 1907. Bill Johnson went to Los Angeles and another Johnson, Nookie Johnson I think, went to L.A. too. Sugar Johnny left early and went to Chicago. Manuel Perez and Arnold Metoyer went up. Freddie Keppard left about 1909. They left because there were more places to work or they just wanted to travel some.

When the District closed in 1914, Joe had taken the Magnolia Band over from Louis Keppard. They had to cut down in the bands, so Joe fired Louis, the bass, and trombone. I'd already left the band by then. The band went right on down after that. Louis kept all the music that belonged to the band. I always tried to get him to give it to me. Way late he told me he got tired of carrying it around and threw it away.

When Pops speaks of his bass playing, he does so in the spirit of the craftsman; his candor stops short of his own accomplishments. Pops Foster was one of the great bassists in jazz and the first of its stylists. Jazz bass playing began with Pops, and, from the band affiliations cited for his early career, it is evident that his services were even then much in demand. Magnolia, Tuxedo, John Robichaux, Armand Piron, Freddie Keppard, Frankie Dusen, and Kid Ory—these were among the leading New Orleans bands of the time; moreover, these affiliations reflect considerable style differences, ranging from the melodious, almost proper dance music of Robichaux to the rough, funky, bluesy style heard in Frankie Dusen's Eagle Band. New Orleans style was taking shape in those years. The vigorous playing of uptown (black) musicians like Keppard and Dusen was gaining in popularity, all the while absorbing the useful elements of the dying Creole tradition.

The first recordings of New Orleans jazz were made in 1917 by the Victor Talking Machine Company, the principal manufacturer of phonographs and records. After surveying the talent field, Victor decided to offer its contract to Freddie Keppard. The bandleader's refusal for fear that other musicians would plagiarize his musical ideas is one of the oldest jazz legends, and is supported by Pops Foster's statements. Victor then offered the same contract to a competent but by no means outstanding white group led by Nick La Rocca and calling itself the Original Dixieland Jazz Band. The style is considered derivative by most jazz writers. Thus the first but by no means definitive jazz records were made on February 24, 1917, in New York City, there being no adequate recording facilities in New Orleans. The first Victor release, on the old 78-rpm ten-inch disc format, was "Dixie Jazz Band One-Step" backed by "Livery Stable Blues"—not actually a blues, but a novelty number with minstrel show overtones, spiced by crude imitations of barnyard fauna: hen's cackle (clarinet), mare's whinny (muted cornet), and donkey's bray (trombone). Thus vulgarized, New Orleans jazz was introduced to the American public not as seri-

ous music, but as a novelty. It was an instant success. The Original Dixieland Jazz Band was signed to a long-term Victor recording contract and embarked upon a series of lucrative bookings that eventually took ODJB to London. The exploitation of African-American musical ideas by white imitators, long the complaint of black jazzmen, may be said to date from 1917 with Keppard's paranoiac refusal and La Rocca's politic and timely handling of the opportunity to make the first records. Later Keppard had reason to regret his decision. Keppard recorded in Chicago in 1923, but for independent record labels and as a featured trumpeter in bands other than his own.

The question arises: What was New Orleans jazz really like? Documentation of the real thing waited until 1923, when the recording industry—independents as well as major labels—suddenly awoke to the sales potential offered by the jazz and blues market. By 1923 many of the leading New Orleans bands were working in Chicago, where studio facilities existed. Among those who made records at this time were Keppard, King Oliver (Oliver's Creole Jazz Band with the Dodds brothers and Louis Armstrong), Clarence Williams (with Sidney Bechet), and Jelly Roll Morton. Pops Foster first recorded in 1924 in St. Louis for Okeh, with Charlie Creath's Jazz-O-Maniacs. Due to the limitations of prewar engineering techniques, several records made after World War II offer the best examples of Pops's playing.

The more representative recordings of New Orleans jazz in its purest state are the King Oliver Creole Jazz Band titles originally made for Gennett. That company went into bankruptcy during the Depression of the '30s, but the titles have been reissued. New Orleans jazz was characterized by flowing rhythm, usually 4/4; emphasis on melody rather than harmonic embellishment; simple forms, most often 12- and 16-bar, derived from blues, ragtime, and marching band music; and free polyphony. Polyphony was created by the constant interweaving and intermingling of melodic lines played by the instruments of the front line: cornet, clarinet, and trombone.

—Ross Russell

Chapter 4
Gigging Around

"When we were playing we were having fun;
the pay sometimes just made it a little bit sweeter."

When I was with the Magnolia Band sometimes they didn't play rough enough to suit me. So I'd lay off once in a while on Saturday night and go play with Frankie Dusen's Eagle Band. They were rough babies who drank a lot and really romped. I'd try to dance the quadrilles when they played; I'd run and jump and kick my leg out and have a big time.

From about 1900 on, there were three types of bands around New Orleans. You had bands that played ragtime, ones that played sweet music, and the ones that played nothin' but blues. A band like John Robichaux's playing nothin' but sweet music and played the dicty affairs. On a Saturday night, Frankie Dusen's Eagle Band would play the Masonic Hall because he played a whole lot of blues. A band like the Magnolia Band would play ragtime and work the District. They'd play "Bag of Rags," "Frog Leg Rag," "Maple Leaf Rag," "Champagne Rag," and ones like that; they were all dance numbers. All the bands around New Orleans would play quadrilles starting about midnight. When you did that, nice people would know it was time to go home because things got rough after that. The rough guys would come about midnight. They were pimps, whores, hustlers, and that bunch. They'd dance with no coats on and their suspenders down. They'd jump around and have a bunch of fun. They wanted you to play slow blues and dirty songs so they could dance rough and dirty. On the boats when they got to dancing that way you had to shoot a waltz in. Sometimes it was so rough you played waltzes back to back. Back in those days I thought it was rough stuff, but today I see where they were just having fun.

None of the bands around New Orleans had singers. The only singer around was Willie Jackson. He and a guy named Nookey had a black-faced comedian act. Willie could sing pretty good. Most of the guys you heard singing down there were guys who came out of the woods somewhere with a guitar playing and singing the blues.

There were three sections of New Orleans and a lot of districts. There was Uptown, Downtown, and Back of Town. The Downtown boys, the Creoles, thought they were better than anybody else and wouldn't hire the Uptown boys. Most of the guys who played the District were from Downtown. Some of the Downtown bands were the Imperial Band, the Superior Band, and the Olympic Band. The Uptown musicians had the biggest names, Buddy Bolden's band and Kid Ory's Band. Bolden's band had the biggest name around there for a long time. There used to be a lot of German bands come into New Orleans on the boats, and they'd go all over town playing and serenading people. People would throw money down to them for playing. The German bands came before the war, and when the war started they quit comin'. Most of them had baritone horns, trumpets, bass drums, trombone, and alto horn.

The rich people who lived in Audubon Place were always throwing affairs we'd play. Those people would never ask how much the band was, they'd just tell you to come on such and such a night. We knew when they didn't ask we'd get more than we usually made when you told them the price. In the summertime, the rich men would send their wives and children away for vacation and then throw big parties all the time they were gone. They'd have girls, party and dance all night long. Sometimes they'd hire a barge and a tugboat for pulling it out in the lake to party. They'd stay out there all night having their party while we played. The drunker they got the more they'd tip. They wouldn't know a five from a one.   •

The rich also had places especially built for their kids to have dances. Like a big house would be on one corner, and another on the next corner. Then in the middle of the block there'd be a little dance hall for the kids. We played a lot of gigs in those places. The rich also had music at the Audubon Club, the City Golf Club, and the West End Golf Club.

John Robichaux got most of the dicty jobs like that around town. He had the rich people's jobs all sewed up for a long time. His band played the country clubs, restaurants like Antoine's or Gallatoire's where the rich people gave dinners and had dancing, private clubs like Jackson Square Gardens or the Harmony Club where they'd have parties. John was a big shot and hardly spoke to anybody. He got the best jobs around, and when you hired the John Robichaux Band you had the cream of the crop. Robichaux's band played only what was written, but they did play some of the Scott Joplin tunes, and if you played what he wrote you played enough. John had the best reading band in town. He wouldn't hire anyone who couldn't read. I played with Robichaux's band for a while.

Robichaux was a left-handed violin player and his band played mostly sweet music. For a long time they had the only piano player with a band; it was a woman whose name I can't remember. The other guys in his band were James Williams, cornet; Baptiste DeLisle, trombone; Coochie Martin, guitar; Walter Brundy, drums; and George Baquet, clarinet.

There were other guys who played with Robichaux, though. Bud Scott played guitar with Robichaux's band early. He left New Orleans around 1905 and went to New York. He played around New York with Jim Europe and some of those guys. For a while there he'd go back and forth quite a bit. When I went to Los Angeles in 1922 to join Ory he was with Ory. Bud wasn't much of a jazzman. He played mostly pop numbers and was a good rhythm man. Johnny St. Cyr also played guitar with Robichaux. Johnny was a good rhythm man too and wasn't any jazz player.

There were only two drummers around town who could read music, Walter Brundy and Zutty Singleton. Walter was the best drummer and reader. When Walter left for Chicago about 1918 or 1919, Zutty started playing with Robichaux.

For years the guys in Robichaux's band didn't speak to each other. It's the only band I ever saw like that. Those Frenchmen get mad at you and just quit speaking. The guys would pass around the music to each other and play together, but wouldn't speak. They were all mad at each other. Ory's band was like that for a while.

Way late around New Orleans the dicty people got tired of hearing that violin scratchin' all night and start to hire some bands who'd play some rough music for them. Jack Carey's band, the Tuxedo Band, and some others who could read and play some sweet music too started getting some of the jobs. The Magnolia Band and the Superior Band could play anything, too. The bands that couldn't read made the most money and were the biggest talk of the town. They were gutbucket bands like Ory's band and for a while Dusen's Eagle Band. They played hot all the time.

The other best-reading band around New Orleans was Bab Frank's Peerless Band. Bab played very nice piccolo and a little clarinet. "High Society" was a piccolo solo, and Bab played it very good. The only guy who could play it on E-flat clarinet was Picou. Most of the guys played E-flat in the bands and used a different clarinet to play in the brass bands. Big Eye Louis played a C clarinet so he could read the violin parts.

Bab was always starting trouble with the girls in the District. When he'd see a bunch of them standing around he'd say, "You whores ought to get yourselves an honest job, you bunch of bitches." They'd call him all kinds of names, and one that stuck on him was "Lump of Corruption." The guys started calling him that. The last time I saw Bab was in 1928 in San Francisco's Third Street Station. I was on my way to Chicago with the Elk's Brass Band and he was working as a Red Cap. He was gonna come around that night where we were playing, but he didn't show up.

Bab had a nice band and a very good trumpet player, Andrew Kimball. Vic Gaspard played trombone; Charlie McCurdy, clarinet; Oke Gaspard (Vic's brother), string bass; Coochie White, guitar; Jean Vigne, drums; and Bab's brother Alcide played violin. Vic Gaspard was a nice old guy and one of the best trombone players we had around New Orleans.

On the stand Vic would go to sleep. The band would knock off and he'd start right along with them, make all the breaks, and lay his horn on his lap when he finished. If you'd wake him up he'd grab his horn and come in in the wrong place.

I worked once in a while with Bab's band to take Oke's place. This would usually happen when there were two bands on a date. Oke would say, "Hey, Georgie, I want you to play a couple of numbers for me, I'll be right back." I'd get up on the stand with Bab's band. Oke would take off and wouldn't come back. When you'd see him next time he'd say, "You know, man, I didn't even think about coming back, I just forgot." Or, "Man, I couldn't get away, I had a lot of business to take care of." This happened with a lot of other guys too, and I did it myself, so nobody thought anything about it. All that happened was, you'd found a hot chick and you wanted to take off with her. It was more kicks than work to play with both bands all night.

Alcide and Bab played in the Edward Clem Band before they had their own band. That was way early when I first started in the District. In those days the violin was usually the leader. What that means was he called the numbers, stomped off, and played the violin as the lead instrument. Alcide was the leader of Clem's band. Bab played piccolo and some clarinet in the band. Edward Clem was a very good trumpet player and was the manager. Miles Ross played bass; Spencer Jackson, guitar; a guy named "Sugah" on trombone; and a drummer that I can't remember—he drank so much they had to put him out of the band. The band played the Funky Butt Hall on Saturday night.

Frankie Dusen's Eagle Band played the Masonic Dance Hall and the Eagle Saloon. The Saloon was at Perdido and Rampart streets, and that's where the band got its name from. They even played there when it was Buddy Bolden's band. We used to call them "the Boys in Brown"

because they had regular brown military uniforms with caps that had their names on them.

There were a lot of different guys who played in the Eagle Band. Dandy Lewis was the bass player until he blew his top. Then Bob Lyons was with them. He had his room right over the Eagle Saloon. If you picked up a chick there, you rented Bob's room for a quarter. You'd take her upstairs, knock out, and then go on home. There were a gang of trumpet players in the Eagle Band. John Penerton was the first one I remember after Bolden, then Wild Ned was next. Both of them played what they could see and played very good. I wouldn't call them hot players though. Then they got Bunk Johnson. Bunk claims he played with Bolden, but he was in the Superior Band when Bolden was around, and I played with them. The first time I saw Bunk was at the Fairgrounds at a big picnic in 1908. There were three bands playing: John Robichaux's band was in the pavilion, I was with Manuel Perez's brass band playing dance music outside, and the Superior Band was out on the racetrack and were playing for people to dance on the grass. The Superior Band was a ragtime band. They had Bunk; Buddy Johnson, trombone; Peter Bocage, violin; Rene Baptiste, guitar; Billy Moran, bass; Big Eye Louis, clarinet; and Walter Brundy, drums. Bunk played a beautiful horn, and nobody else around New Orleans played the same style Bunk did. He played the most beautiful tones. After a while Bunk got to drinking so bad they fired him, and then he went with Frankie Dusen's band.

Frankie Dusen was the only guy that Bunk was afraid of and who could make Bunk listen. Bunk would show up to play so drunk he'd be draggin' his coat across the floor and couldn't find the bandstand. He'd try to put his horn up to his mouth and hit his nose or chin and couldn't even find his mouth. When he was like that or just passed out, the guys would say to him, "Hey Bunk, here comes Frankie." Bunk would straighten right up. The reason was Frankie used to beat Bunk just like you beat a kid. He'd get a razor strap or his belt and whip him.

Bunk was a very nice guy when he was in the Superior Band, but when he went with the Eagle Band he really got to drinking bad. In those days the saloons never closed and Bunk never left the Eagle Saloon. He'd drink till he passed out and then sleep it off on a pool table, get up, and start drinking again. If we came along and wanted to shoot pool, we'd just lift Bunk off and lay him on a bench. He got to drinking so bad that even the Eagle Band fired him about 1910 and no one else would hire him. He left town with a minstrel show, and I didn't see him again until 1937 when I was playing with Louis Armstrong's band in New Iberia, Louisiana. Bunk claimed he got Louis his first job, but Bunk wasn't even around New Orleans when Johnny Dodds and Peter Bocage got Louis the job with Fate Marable on the boats. Until that, Louis just had one-night gigs with different bands.

After the Eagle Band fired Bunk they got Joe Oliver, but he quit and came to the Magnolia Band. Joe Johnson, who was with us in the Rozelle Band, took Oliver's place. I think drinking with all the heavy drinkers in the band half killed Joe Johnson. He, Joe Penerton, and Wild Ned all died young of TB after playing with the Eagle Band. Joe left the Eagle Band too and went with Jack Carey's band until he died in about 1914.

I went to Joe's funeral with the four Dutrey Brothers. All of us used to come around the church when Joe was singing in the choir and get him out to play jobs. We'd signal him we needed him to play; he'd drop out of the choir and come with us. At the funeral the preacher was really mad at us and thought we'd caused Joe to die. He started talking about how Joe was a good church man and how we pulled him out of church. He really started laying it on us. I remember him yelling, "*and* they're here right now—one of them carries a string bass around on his back and it's the devil riding his back." He was sure talking to us. None of the guys played trumpet like Joe. He played the middle range and played it rough and beautiful.

Frankie Dusen was a slick guy with the girls. He was a tall, good-looking guy with straight hair and kind of dark. Out in the little country towns the straighter your hair was, the more the girls went for you. Every time Frankie would play out in the country he'd carry some girl back to New Orleans with him or have her follow him. There was always some country girl coming around who'd left home and was looking for Frankie to stay with. He'd let them stay with him until he got tired of them, then he'd send them home. He wasn't married as long as I was around there.

One night Frankie and I went over to Pearl River, Mississippi, to play a date with a local band at a tenant farm town. After we finished we went to wait for the ferry to carry us to the train that took us back to New Orleans. At the ferry landing two tough guys with pistols caught us. They wanted us to drink with them and play the string bass and trombone. Frankie was always sick, but he was sicker than usual and wasn't supposed to do any drinking. I tried to talk them out of making Frankie drink, but they just said, "It won't do him no harm," and kept telling him, "Come on and drink, big boy." So we drank and played, and they put their pistols away. It didn't seem to do Frankie any harm. Mississippi was a dry state, but they had the best corn whiskey in the world there.

The only musician I ever had a fight with was Emile Bigard while I was playing with Ory's band. Emile was a nice guy and a very good violin player. We were always friends before and after that. Ory's band had a job up around Ory's home, and I was playing it with him. After the job was over the band was riding back home in a closed wagon. There was a curtain over the back. I wanted the curtain down so I could sleep and Emile wanted it up for fresh air. I put it down and he put it back up. I hit him and knocked him down and that was all of the fight. I was very sorry about it. When we were both in the Magnolia Band we used to rehearse at his daddy's house. Barney Bigard was a little tiny guy then. He used to come around and pull our music off the stands.

There were a lot of players around New Orleans who would only play with their own band. Some of the guys were Ory, Frankie Dusen, Albert Nicholas, and George Brunies. Those guys couldn't read so good or couldn't read at all, and they couldn't go into other bands and start playing. Ory couldn't read too good and couldn't find a note either. If he wanted B-flat he couldn't slide up to it and blow, he'd have to slur his horn up to it. He'd stop when he got on the note. I was always able to play with any band by reading or playing by head. That's the way I played with so many bands around town. The toughest thing to play is music for toe dancing. Man, it goes so fast and has to be right on time when those toes touch the floor. They tell you you've got to hit it right with the catch. I remember once when they told Zutty Singleton to hit it on the drums when the man caught the girl. Zutty hit it, but both of them were clear off the stage when he went *bang*. Very few jazz musicians can play for toe dancing.

Johnny Dodds didn't read so good, and the only band he had played with was Ory's. When work got tough he was talking about going to St. Louis or Chicago and wanted to know if I thought he could play with the other bands. I told him he should study and train himself to play with any band and not just one like he'd done. I also told him that if he could play with a band in New Orleans, he could play with the bands up there. He said, "Yeah, George, that's what I did wrong, I got wrapped up around one band and I sound funny with anybody else." After that he studied and could play with all bands.

About 1914 I was playing with Ory's band doing advertising for an affair the Turtles [social club] were putting on at National Park. That was the ballpark at Third and Willow. Chiff Matthews was playing trumpet; he was a little bitty guy and played good trumpet. His brother Stone Matthews was playing guitar, and he was a fine player. Stone was a heavy drinker and would get sloppy drunk. He was sloppy drunk that day and Ory told him to get out of the wagon and go home. Stone got out and Chiff did too. So then we needed a trumpet player very bad. After we went a few blocks, I saw Louis Armstrong standing on a corner watching, and said, "Hey, there's little Louis over there!" We got him in the wagon, and he went on to play the advertising with us, and then we carried him out to the park to play. The only thing Louis could play then was blues, so we played them all day long. Louis played them good too. As far as I know, that was the first time Louis played with a big-time band. Before that Louis just played with kid bands.

Chiff and Stone Matthews never did play in Ory's band again. Stone drank himself to death right after that, and Chiff didn't play too much after that. Chiff played string bass too, and when I went back to New Orleans in 1937 he was playing string bass with a little band around there. Up until Ory's band most of the bands had names like Crescent Band, Silver Leaf Band, Eagle Band, and so on. The only bands I can remember who used guys names were John Robichaux's Band and Buddy Bolden's Band. Ory started playing in New Orleans around 1906 and was a hot baby around town. People liked his music, and it was very hot. His band could play a waltz and make it hot. He made such a big hit that all the other bands started changing the names of their band to the leaders name to copy Ory. The Crescent Band be-came Jack Carey's Band, the Silver Leaf Band started being called Albert Baptiste's Band, the Young Olympia Band became Ernest John-son's Young Olympia—there were four or five Olympia bands around there. Ory's band would have still been going strong today if he had-n't let his wife run his band.

Eddie Garland—we always called him Montudie—was always fighting with Ory, so I'd go play with Ory's band and Montudie would play with the Magnolia Band until they started getting along again. A lot of us guys would trade off among bands to take out-of-town jobs. Whoever didn't have a day job, or could make it, would go. Montudie started with Ory about 1908, and those guys played and fought to-gether nearly all their lives.

I got Johnny Dodds his first job around New Orleans with Ory about 1908. Johnny was working at the rice mill, and at noon they'd stop for lunch. He would come out on the road to sit and eat his lunch and practice blowing his clarinet. I'd be driving by in a wagon and I'd stop to listen to him play. After I heard him several times out on the road, I asked him if he wanted a job playing in a band. He said he did, so I met him that night and carried him down to Globe's Hall where Ory was playing. He played with the band and Ory liked the way he did, so he hired him. Ory's band was the only one Johnny played with until he left New Orleans.

Not too long after Johnny got the job with Ory, he got salty with me because I wouldn't go with Ory's band and went with Joe Oliver instead. Johnny wanted to get rid of Montudie and wanted me to take the job. But Montudie and I were great friends, and I wouldn't take a job from him. We are still great friends, and he's one of the last of the New Orleans guys. The only time we'd take each other's jobs was when we were having rough times with our own band and wanted to get out for a while. I've heard people say Johnny was mean, but he wasn't. Sidney Bechet and Leadbelly are a couple of mean babies, but not Johnny. I used to visit him and his wife in Chicago years later. I knew her before he did and used to try to check in on her.

The guys around New Orleans used to call Johnny "Toilet." The guys in Ory's band started it but all of us picked it up. The whole Dodds family was short, and they all had bad hearts. It seems like the whole family died of heart trouble.

Before Johnny Dodds went with Ory, their clarinet player was Johnny Brown. He also played violin. Once he got started playing his clarinet, he couldn't stop, he just couldn't make no ending. When you got to the end of a number, you'd reach over and pull the clarinet out of his mouth so he'd stop. After I carried Johnny Dodds to Ory, Johnny Brown went to violin. Him and Dodds sat beside each other in Ory's band for years and never spoke to each other.

William Ridgley was the leader of the Tuxedo Band. I got Papa Celestin his first real job playing with them before they left the Tuxedo Dance Hall. That was back about 1909 or 1910. Back in those days we called him Sonny, and that's what I still call him; way late they started calling him Papa. Sonny was working for the Texas and Pacific Railroad making $1.25 a day and gigging around with different bands. I used to go over to his house and hang around waiting for him to come home. I'd cut wood so his wife could fix his dinner. One day they needed a trumpet player in the Tuxedo Band, and I came to tell him to go down. He didn't want to go; he was afraid that he'd lose his job on the railroad. Finally he decided to take it. The last time I saw him around New York we were talking about it, and he said he wished he'd quit and gone to work in the District a long time before he did.

The Tuxedo Band had William Ridgley—we called him Bebe—playing trombone; Sam Dutrey, clarinet; Sonny, cornet; Ernest "Quank" Trippania, drums. Johnny Lindsay played bass; later he took up trombone and turned out to be a real nice trombone player. His brother Herbert played violin in the band. Herb played a whole lot of jazz like Stuff Smith, and he was very good. Herb was a mean guy who was always getting into some kind of trouble, and he looked just like me. The cops were always picking me up for his trouble, but I knew the station cops and they knew him, so they'd let me go. He had a beautiful wife, and sometimes she'd come to dances we were playing. If she danced twice with the same guy, Herb would get off the stand and take her home. My brother used to do the same thing. They were a bunch of jealous babies.

It was a rule in New Orleans if you didn't play any blues you didn't get any colored jobs, and if you didn't play lancers you didn't get Cajun jobs. White jobs didn't care what you played. The Tuxedo Band didn't play any blues; they were a ragtime band and didn't get colored jobs. They got a lot of the show jobs and later on some of the dicty affairs.

⁂

I played some with Freddie Keppard before he left New Orleans. Freddie played what I called a walking trumpet. It was *tata-ta-ta-ta*. They were straight clear notes. When Freddie left in 1909 he took five guys with him: Eddie Vinson, trombone; Big Eye Louis Nelson, clarinet; a guy named Clerk on piano; Jimmie Palao on violin; Dink Johnson was their first drummer, then they had a guy named Mac. Up North all the bands had to use piano. Clerk got sick and died. They needed another piano player so they sent for Fess Manetta to go up and join them. Freddie was the first guy to go North with a whole band and play. They played at the Palace Theatre first, and they had that job booked before they left. When they got up there they found the field was so big they started booking three or four jobs a night. They'd play two hours one place, then go on to another and play two hours. Chicago paid more than New Orleans, and those guys were doing great. It wasn't long before the New Orleans guys were taking all the work away from the Chicago musicians. They were so popular the union had to give them a card. Freddie and his Creole Band really opened up Chicago for the rest of the guys to go.

Freddie also had the first chance to record, but passed it up because he was afraid other guys would steal his stuff. Instead the Dixieland Band did, and that's how ragtime music got the Dixieland name. The guys called Dixieland players today think the louder you play, the better you are. Most of them are just loud. Back in the early days we used to play soft and hot. Most of the time it was so quiet you could hear the people's feet shufflin' on the floor.

Freddie was a big guy when he was in New Orleans, but he wasn't fat. After he went North he started drinking a lot and put on whiskey fat. Freddie left when I was playing the District. One of the last jobs we played was a banquet at Perseverance Hall on Berry Street. The societies would have them on Mondays to get new members. They would lay out a big table a block long full of meat and all kinds of food, and they'd have a barrel of wine and a couple kegs of beer. There was no whiskey unless you brought it yourself, and everybody waited on themselves. You only got a dollar for playing one, but you got all you could eat. Freddie, George Baquet, and I were in the band that played that banquet.

The last job I played with Freddie was a Labor Day parade. The parade was put on by the longshoreman's union. They had white unions and colored unions; each one had their own parade and picnic. For the parade all of you just got out in the street and played and marched. The union followed along behind you, and up front the grand marshal led you. Freddie and I were playing in Jack Carey's Brass Band; Freddie was on trumpet and I was on bass drum. The old guys in the brass bands would make the new players play the bass drum to get their rhythm, and most of the drummers around New Orleans started on bass drum in a brass band. The only drummer out of New Orleans that never had much rhythm was Zutty Singleton. Zutty was a hardheaded guy who was headstrong and would never listen. He was always wanting to fight about something, but he never did. He just wanted to make a big disturbance.

Back in those early days we used to do a lot of funny things, like when one of the bands would be playing and a good-looking chick would come in the place, one of the guys would say, "Gee, I know she's got good bread." Then someone else would sing it, and pretty soon the whole band would be romping along playing and singing, "Gee, I know she's got good bread." It meant she's got good pussy. We used to do a lot of things like that. Another one was, when you'd leave the stand you'd say, "Don't kill me when I'm out." Sometimes they'd pick up on that and sing it. It meant don't drink the bottle up while I'm gone.

There was so much work around New Orleans, it's tough to remember it all. It seems like there was always some new kind of job we were goin' on. One of the darndest was on a boat going to British Honduras around 1914 to play for the passengers. We took a five-piece band of the four Dutrey brothers and myself. Honoré was on trombone; Jimmy, drums; Pete, violin; Sam, clarinet; and me on bass. We only got as far as Spanish Honduras and they turned us around and ran us back to the States. They wouldn't even let us off the boat; we unloaded our cargo, loaded up with rock ballast, and started back. We didn't have any idea why we were sent back until we got to the jetty in New Orleans. Then the river pilot got on and told us it was because Germany was blowing up all the boats coming out of New Orleans.

We were scared then. During the rest of the war we'd load up boats with mules, horses, and things, then the Germans would sink them right out of New Orleans; it was something brutal.

Another kind of job we used to get was on train excursions on Sundays. They were run by the Southern Pacific and the New Orleans and Great Northern railroads. It cost a dollar for the trip. You'd load up about nine in the morning and ride until 11 in the morning when you'd be at Homer, Breakaway, Thibodaux, or White Castle, Louisiana. The train would pull off on a siding there, and you'd stay there the rest of the day. The band would play, the people would picnic and dance under the trees, and everybody would have a lot of good times. At six in the evening the train would start blowing its whistle. Everybody would load back in the train and head back for New Orleans. It took a long time to get everybody out of the woods, then we'd make a lot of little stops so you'd get in about 11 at night. The band would play going out and until six in the evening, but we'd sleep or party after that.

We used to have a club of musicians at the Twenty-five Saloon before we'd go to work and after we'd get off. There was Freddie Keppard, Jimmie Palao, Eddie Vinson, myself, and a couple of other guys. When we'd get off work we'd buy six drinks all at once for each of us. We'd drink them and then go leapin' off home. Only sometimes we'd have to help each other out of the place. Most of the time after everyone met at the Twenty-five Club, we'd start home. Usually we'd stop off at whoever's house we came to first and stay there till 6:00 A.M., when the saloons opened. At six we'd cut out for the saloon to have one last taste before bed. Sometimes we'd end up staying together until 6:00 P.M. that evening, when we had to start getting ready to go to work. One of the things we used to do for each other was go around to your house and serenade you if it was your birthday. We'd go over after work at 3:00 A.M. or 4:00 A.M. and play numbers we knew you liked. The neighbors liked it too. A lot of times we'd go serenade good customers, or people we just liked. If a guy was building a house, we'd show up and play and help him build it. When we were playing we were having fun; the pay sometimes just made it a little bit sweeter.

Easter Sunday was the biggest day of the year. You'd be hired for one year to the next to play it, and you made more money than any other day. In the day you'd play a picnic and at night you'd have another job playing a dance. New Year's Eve was nothing. Everybody was Catholic and all the saloons were closed, so you went to sleep. Out in the Garden District there was a bunch of Irish guys who called themselves the Buzzards who used to give lawn parties. They used to wear blackface and dress up like buzzards on Mardi Gras day. The Odd Fellows had a parade they held on the tenth of May we used to play. That was Odd Fellows Day.

No matter what dance hall or affair you were playing in New Orleans you stopped for an hour at midnight and had dinner. Whoever was having the dance fed the musicians. Usually you'd have a big plate of gumbo, rice, and French bread. Gumbo was just a pot of water with okra, onions, and celery that you boiled. Then you'd put in the meaty parts of crab all cracked up and add cut-up chicken, ham, sausage, oysters, shrimp, or any other kind of meat you wanted to. You let that baby boil down till it's thick, then serve it with salt and pepper on it. Then you eat. At the dances they'd usually have a whole washtub of gumbo, a huge pile of rice, and all the French bread you could eat. When you ate your midnight dinner you'd usually go down the street or around the corner and find musicians in another band to talk to. Back then you never talked about music when you were away from it. Most of the time you talked about parties, booze, and chicks.

All the musicians ate good at rehearsals too. Everybody wanted you to rehearse at their house so they could have some fun; it would be just like a lawn party. They'd have beans and rice, gumbo, a keg of beer, or a half keg of claret wine. We'd start rehearsing about eight o'clock in the evening and play till 11 or midnight, according to when the juice ran out. You'd be rehearsing inside and people would be dancing outside. After we'd play a number three or four times we didn't need the music anymore. Everybody who played in New Orleans had to memorize. I can still remember a lot of numbers we played back in 1909. I hear one bar of it and I'm ready to romp.

⚜

Continuing with his story, Pops describes the everyday events that were accompanied by live music in New Orleans. In those years there were no radio, no sound movies, no TV, no phonograph records; indeed, no sound-amplifying equipment. Music was the product of flesh-and-blood musicians. Bands were hired for informal affairs as casually as one engages a caterer today. As an omnipresent part of life in New Orleans, music was fittingly present at wakes and funerals. The city contained a number of fraternal organizations that functioned as burial societies, taking care of the final expenses of their members and seeing to the proper interment of the deceased. Musically these were impressive affairs. The coffin was carried to the cemetery followed by one or more bands moving with slow step and playing a dead march. At the burying ground, the band played a hymn or gospel song while the coffin was being lowered into the ground or, as was more often the case in the marshy terrain of the Delta, being placed in the family vault. Immediately following the interment, the band struck up the most lively of tunes, "Didn't He Ramble" ("Oh, he rambled all around, all around the town, till the butchers cut him down . . .") and, with this as the theme, marched in quick-step time back to town where drinking, feasting, and revelry often followed "as the deceased would have wanted it."

That great raconteur of New Orleans mores, Ferdinand "Jelly Roll" Morton, has discoursed at length on the New Orleans funeral on his Library of Congress recordings. The music of the dead march and the playing of such hymns on "Nearer My God to Thee" and "Didn't He Ramble" have been re-created successfully on photograph recordings. In a little-known interview, Louis Armstrong described the excitement of New Orleans funeral music:

> McDonald Cemetery was just about a mile away from where the Black Diamonds, my team, was playing the Algiers team. Whenever a funeral from New Orleans had a body to be buried in the McDonald Cemetery, they would have to cross the

Canal Street ferryboat and march down the same road right near our ball game. Of course when they passed us playing a slow funeral march, we only paused with the game and tipped our hats as to pay respect. When the last of the funeral passed we would continue the game. The game was in full force when the Onward Band was returning from the cemetery. After they had put the body in the ground, they were swingin' "It's a Long Way to Tipperary." They were swinging so good until Joe Oliver reached into the high register beating out those high notes in very fine fashion. And broke our ball (game). Yeah! The players commenced to dropping bats and balls, etc., and we all followed them, all the way back to the New Orleans side and to their destination." [Louis Armstrong interview, "Scanning the History of Jazz," Jazz Review, July 1960]

Brass bands were also in great demand at street parades and carnivals. By the turn of the century, New Orleans parade music had broken away from its formal 6/8 meter, inherited from the old French and German marching bands of colonial days, and become a jazzed music. New time signatures, cross-riffing, countermelodies, and the inevitable polyphony had transformed the old styles into a new kind of music that was unique in America, or for that matter, the world. When a number of bands participated in parades on more important holidays, these affairs became a kind of musical tournament in which the merits of the rival organizations were judged by the crowds.

—Ross Russell

Chapter 5
Lawn Parties and Funerals

"No matter how much of a bum a guy was,
his friends would pass a cup to get money for
a funeral when he quit the scene."

❦

Joe Sullivan was the union leader for the longshoreman, and he had all the best musicians working on longshore work. That's what I did most of the time I wasn't playing. Joe lived out in the Irish Channel and would throw lawn parties on Monday nights. He'd ask the guys who worked for him to come out and play. He always had the best band and would draw a big crowd. Joe took care of us, and if a good boat was coming in he'd send word around to the guys to come to work. If a ship needed tying up, it took about ten minutes and you got paid for a half a day at 40 cents an hour. Joe tried to play string bass, but he wasn't any good.

The colored musicians in New Orleans didn't have no union, but man, we stuck together. Like if we had a job playing the St. Charles Hotel alternating with Bab Frank's band and it was Babs time to go on and Oke Gaspard, his bass player, he hadn't shown up, I'd go right over and start playing with them until he showed up. He'd do the same thing for me. The guys never tried to cut each other's throat; it was better in those days without no union. In New Orleans the colored bands had most of the work.

The whites had a musicians' union, and my cousin Dave Perkins was president of it. They didn't know he was colored. He played tuba and trombone, taught music, and lent out instruments. He played with all of the white bands. The white union would book colored bands on a job with a white band if someone wanted one. A lot of times the white bandleader would be the man who booked you. Many times the Brunies Band would have a job for another band and they would call us. They'd also use Jack Carey's band, Amos Riley's band, or someone else. The Dixieland band in those days was a mixed band, and nobody paid any attention. The leader was Larry Shields, and you had Achille Baquet, George Baquet's brother, playing with them. He was colored and went all over with them. Shields, Brown, Fisher, and the band went on to New York and made some records and were the first New Orleans musicians to do that. That's how everyone got to calling our music Dixieland, because of the name of their band. Their band was one of the hottest white bands around New Orleans. Leon Rappolo lived about a block from me, and I knew him and Shields, Fisher, and Tom Brown. They used to play with eight pieces sometimes and had a baritone horn then.

Out at the Halfway House they had white bands. After a while the Brunies Band got that job. They played for a lot of dances all around New Orleans where I'd be on the same bill with them. The last time I played on a bill with them I was with Amos Riley's band and we were playing at a country picnic out of Bay St. Louis, Mississippi. I missed the train with the other guys and had to get a later one. When I got to Bay St. Louis I hired a wagon for 50 cents to carry me out to the picnic. When I arrived they weren't there, and I started eating sandwiches, having some drinks, and having a good time. When Amos's and Brunies's bands arrived they were sure surprised to see me. They'd gotten lost and couldn't find the place. The Brunies and their band played very good.

Johnny Lala had a white band around New Orleans. His daddy owned the French Market. He played trumpet in the band and was very good. Tony Parenti was another Frenchman, a Cajun guy that had a band. It was one of the best white bands. Tony could read very good, and I was on some of his records way late. He left New Orleans and went to Chicago. He loved to gamble and got in trouble with the big gamblers in Chicago, so he skipped to New York. After a while he got in trouble in New York and left for Florida. He got too slick there too and came back to New York. Tony will see you walkin' down the street and bet you you can't walk. If you play cards or dice with him you've got to keep your eyes on him or he'll slick you.

In New Orleans the colored had Lincoln Park and the whites had White City Park where a big brass band played. The band had two drums—a snare drum and a big bass drum. They played marches and things like that.

None of the white bands had any violin, guitar, mandolin, or string bass. Only the colored played them. Lately a guy down there named Souchon has been saying he played guitar with white bands down there. I never heard of him and I never heard of any white guitar players around New Orleans. The first white guitar players I saw were Eddie Lang and Dick McDonough way late when I was in New York. The white and colored musicians around New Orleans all knew each other, and there weren't any Jim Crow between them. They really didn't much care what color you were, and I played with a lot of them around New Orleans.

Every saloon in New Orleans had a shed on the front and a bench under it. There was a board nailed up out there where they hung coffee cans up. If you wanted a drink you'd pull one down and rinse it out, then go in and get it filled with beer. That was a "can of beer" in those days, and it cost you ten cents. When you got through drinking it, you'd hang it up. At lunch time, three or four guys would buy a can of beer and pass it around. In those days the Italians owned nearly all the grocery stores and saloons. When I worked doing longshore work we used to hang out at Tony's Saloon at Celeste and Chapatula. It was strictly for colored. Most saloons had two sides, one for whites and one for colored. The colored had so much fun on their side dancing, singing, and guitar playing, that you couldn't get in for the whites. It was the same way at Lincoln Park for the colored; you couldn't tell who it was for, there were so many whites there.

There were a lot of dance halls around New Orleans. The Love and Charity Hall was way up on Carlton near Eagle and Poplar. St. Dominic's Hall was on Maple, two blocks from Carlton Street. Elizabeth's Hall was at Camp and Fallon streets; it wasn't a very big hall and we'd play it on Monday nights. All over town they had lawn parties. There was a lot of them in Niggertown; that didn't mean what it does today. A lot of colored lived there, but most of the people weren't colored. It was just a place to us, and I lived there for a while and so did Brock Mumford, Henry Zeno, and Joe Johnson. In the Greenville District out on Carlton there were a lot of lawn parties, and in Pensiontown too; that's on Oak at the Protection Levee. Pensiontown was mostly colored. We played the Irish Channel and there were a lot of Irishmen out there. Frankie Dusen lived in the 12th Ward, which was another section of town. On Tuesday nights we used to play for the Bulls Club in the Garden District; they'd have two bands playing. If you joined their club you had your own key, and the club was for gambling and carrying on. The Turtles was a big club and they used to put on dances at the ballpark at Third and Willow. Back of the District was called the Battlefield. When we were kids we used to go back there and pick palms to sell for Easter Sunday. We'd also go there to catch crayfish and pick blackberries.

I met my first wife playing a lawn party out in the Irish Channel and married her in 1912. Her name was Bertha and her folks couldn't stand me. He folks were poor and hated me playin' music for a livin'; they didn't think it was enough for anybody to do. Back then everybody classified musicians as bums, which they were—a musician was just no good. If a girl was with you at a dance nobody would talk to her—she was a bad woman. It was very rough to find a room to rent if you were a musician. I stayed with Bertha about ten years. After we got married, I sent her to school. She got so smart she didn't want to do nothin'. In 1922 I left her for a short trip to Los Angeles to play with Kid Ory and haven't seen her since.

The worst Jim Crow around New Orleans was what the colored did to themselves. The uptown clubs and societies were the strictest. You had to be a doctor or a lawyer or some kind of big shot to get in. The lighter you were the better they thought you were. The Francs Amis Hall was like that. That place was so dicty they wouldn't let us come off the bandstand because we were too dark. They would let the lightest guy in the bandstand go downstairs and get drinks for all of us. They hired one guy they called Foster who entertained them all the time. He was as black as the ace of spades, and he was very smart and spoke eight different languages. When he finished entertaining he had to go into a little room and stay there. Some of the societies were so bad they wouldn't even let black people go in. There was a colored church in town that had seating by color. The lightest ones down in front and darker and darker as you went back. There was a place over in Biloxi, Mississippi, where they had albinos. They had white kinky hair and couldn't see good during the day. We used to play dances for them, but they wouldn't let you into the dance unless you were an albino. The Negro race has always been crazy. They're the most mixed-up race of people you ever saw. You get every color in the Negro race, the skin is different, the eyes, the hair is different color and kinky or not so kinky.

In Washington, D.C., way late I was playing a dance for the colored mint workers and the colored mail carriers. The mint workers were lighter than the mail carriers. They had themselves roped off and wouldn't allow the carriers on their side. We moved the whole band over to the mail carriers' side and told them this was our kind of people over here. That was the only dance I every played where the colored people came on time. Usually colored don't show up at a dance until 11 or 12, and the band starts at eight or nine. You've played your brains out by the time anyone gets there. That's why by the time people show up the guys are all drunked up sometimes. The colored usually stay until three or four in the morning.

A lot of people have talked about the funerals the colored used to have in New Orleans, but they don't mention the wakes. I guess that's because they only saw the funeral going by in the streets. The wakes for the dead were the big thing. They also called the wakes "coffee boats" or just "boats." They'd lay the dead man out in the parlor on what was called a "coolin' board," and everyone would sing hymns over him. You'd drink coffee, beer, wine, and whiskey, and they had sandwiches to eat. Guys who could sing and knew all the hymns were in demand and got invited to all the boats. There were always a couple of guys who hung out with us who could sing the hymns. They'd invite us to the boat to sing, or we'd go and stand outside the window and they'd pass sandwiches out to us. They didn't play any instruments at the wakes, just sing and get drunk. People would get carried away shouting and clapping; the girls would faint because some guy could sing so good. They were just as happy at a time as the march home from the burying. If you went to a wake you couldn't make it to work the next day.

One night we went to a boat for a small guy who'd died. Everybody went to the back of the house to drink and eat and left him alone in the parlor. This woman named Charlotte snuck in the parlor, took the dead man and propped him up in the corner. When we all came back in the parlor he wasn't on the coolin' board. Everybody started looking around for him and then we saw him in the corner. Everybody head for the door and a lot of people got hurt getting out of there. Charlotte was sitting across the street watching everything and laughing. The judge gave her 30 days in jail for hurting the people.

A whole lot has been written about colored funerals in New Orleans. We used to play a funeral two or three times a month. They always buried on Sunday for a long time, then started burying on Mondays. No matter how much of a bum a guy was, his friends would pass a cup to get money for a funeral when he quit the scene. If there was any money after paying for the funeral the widow would get it. The guys would rent a set of tails for the grand marshal, hire a brass band,

and buy some flowers. Going out to the cemetery the band would play hymns like "Nearer My God to Thee" and "When the Saints Go Marching In" very slow. These are hymns and you never played them fast or jazzed them up. You also only played hymns at church services, never in the District. In the '30s when I was in Louis Armstrong's band we nearly got run out of a little town in Texas for playing "When the Saints Go Marching In" at a dance. As soon as they put the guy in the ground, the trumpeter would hit a couple of high notes. When the trumpet hit the last note the bass drum would start off, *boom-boom, boom-boom-boom, boom-boom-boom-boom,* and then everybody would take off on something like "Didn't He Ramble." We'd play jazz music all the way back. I played the string bass in the funerals.

Today guys are always asking me about the funerals and brass bands back then so they can play like them. Up here when they try they always have a guy with cymbals, or a stick, lead the band. In New Orleans the trumpet player led the band. He hit a couple of notes and you get started. Up here someone has to blow a whistle to get them started. All the guys in New Orleans used to wear band uniforms, and they looked very nice. I used to put it on and carry my bass by a strange girl I wanted to meet. That would start her talkin'.

Out on the beaches the colored had their side and the whites theirs. On the train out to West End the train would stop and the colored would get off on one side and the whites on the other. The colored side was Milneburg. At West End and Spanish Fort, which was an amusement park for whites, they hired colored bands.

We'd get a lot of jobs to go out to those little towns in the country. Sometimes they'd hire one or two New Orleans musicians to play with a local band, and sometimes they'd hire our whole band. At the dances in the country or over to Mississippi, white people would come to the colored dances. The whites would sit on the bandstand or in front of it and listen to the music and watch the colored people dance. Sometimes they would have a roped-off section for white spectators, and sometimes we'd play two nights; one for the whites and one for the colored. At colored dances there'd usually be as many whites as colored. Over at Bay St. Louis in Mississippi, we had a sheriff who wanted to go to one of the dances so bad he opened the jail and brought all the prisoners with him. He'd buy the boys beer and gumbo. He said it was one time he could get out and have some fun. The next day going home we saw the sheriff and the prisoners out workin' on the road.

The first time I ever saw a barbecue was at one of those country dances. They dug a hole in the ground just like a grave and put some kind of bark in it that they'd burn down to coals. Then they'd put some metal rods across the top and lay a half a hog on to barbecue. You could smell the meat cooking for miles and miles. You'd get hungry the minute you smelled it. I didn't know what to call it at first so I called it "hog on the ground."

We used to play over in Algiers at the Perseverance Park and the Perseverance Dance Hall. When I was still a kid I had a little thing going on in Algiers with an older woman for a long time. I wanted to fool around with older women then. She was a friend of George Hooker's wife. George was a baritone horn player with the Onward Brass Band, and he had a nice little wife. I used to go to his house a lot when he wasn't home to see his wife's friend. Her husband was a bad man who was a barber. I'd meet her at George's house, then we'd go to the bedroom and do our little business. Then one of us would take off, then the other would take off. I went with her for years. I played a dance at the Perseverance Park every Sunday. Man, they sure had some beautiful women around Algiers.

Once I was playing around Magnolia, Louisiana, and I was walking a local chick home after the dance. We were walking behind these two old hens, and all they could talk about was those bad old musicians and what they did. It gave me fits. Musicians were nowhere in the South. If you'd play a dance in the country, you'd carry a few girls along to entertain at the dance. If any of the local guys would talk to the show girls, the local girls wouldn't have any more to do with them because they'd been out with those bad old show girls. Show people were classified as nothin', and musicians were rotten. They weren't no good either. We did a lot of funny things in those days. We were always being put out of hotels for the stuff we did. All of us made a lot of noise and had a lot of pleasure. We thought it was funny to get put out of a hotel.

In Baton Rouge, Louisiana, there was the Toots Johnson Band. It was very good, and Guy Kelly played trumpet with them. They wanted me to go to Montana with them, but I found out it was very cold there and it was wintertime. I told them I wouldn't go because it was too cold, so they wrote a letter to find out. When they got the answer they found out it was, so they didn't go either.

Over in Bay St. Louis, Mississippi, one time, we were playing advertising for a dance that night. I was on the back of the wagon playing bass, and we went under a low tree. The neck of the bass caught on a limb and we both went swinging out. Then the limb broke. I landed on the bottom and the bass landed on top of me, so neither of us got hurt. Everybody but me laughed their heads off.

Don Redman Orchestra, early 1930s. From left: Sidney de Paris, trumpet; Bennie Morton, trombone; Shirley Clay, trumpet; Fred Robinson, trombone; Manzie Johnson, drums, Langston Curl, trumpet; Claude Jones, trombone; Horace Henderson, piano; Don Redman, saxophone; Edward Inge, reeds; Talcott Reeves, guitar; Bob Carroll, reeds; Bob Ysaquire, bass; Rupert Cole, reeds.

Louis Bacon, about 1930.

Theodore "Teddy" Hill, about 1930.

Luis Russell, about 1930.

Johnny Dodds, about 1928.

Henry "Red" Allen, Jr., about 1930.

Luis Russell and His Famous Orchestra, about 1932. From left: Pops Foster, bass; Luis Russell, piano and leader; Sonny Woods, vocals; Tiny Bradshaw, drums; Henry "Moon" Jones, reeds; Lee Blair, guitar; Charlie Holmes, reeds; Leonard "Ham" Davis, trumpet; Louis Bacon, trumpet; Jimmy Archey, trombone; Gus Aiken, trumpet; Bingie Madison, reeds; Harry "Father" White, trombone.

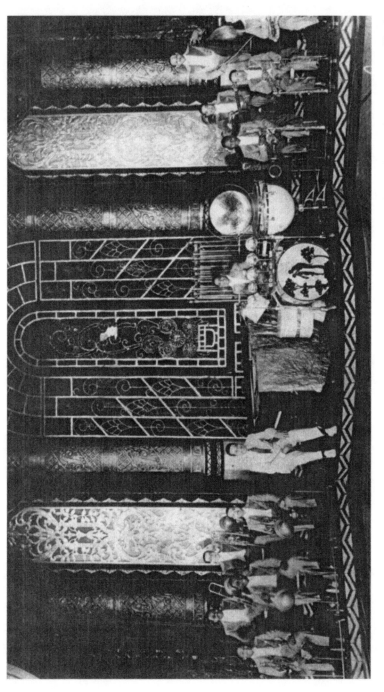

The Duke Ellington Orchestra at the Oriental Theater, Chicago, about 1930. From left: Freddy Jenkins, trumpet; Tricky Sam Nanton, trombone; Cootie Williams, trumpet; Juan Tizol, trombone; Arthur "Chief" Whetzel, trumpet; Duke Ellington, piano and leader; Sonny Greer, drums; Harry Carney, reeds; Fred Guy, guitar; Johnny Hodges, reeds; Wellman Braud, bass; Barney Bigard, reeds.

Earl Hines, about 1930.

Horace Henderson, about 1935.

Fletcher Henderson, about 1933.

James P. Johnson, about 1930.

Thomas Fats Waller, about 1935.

Alma Foster, New York City, about 1930.

❦

"In those days it was called 'ragtime music,'" recalls Louis Armstrong, "and whenever there was a dance or lawn party, the band of six men would stand in front of the place in the sidewalk and play a half hour of good ragtime music." [Louis Armstrong, "Scanning the History of Jazz," Jazz Review, July 1960.]

Pops expands on Armstrong's idea. Piano ragtime composers like Scott Joplin and James Scott wrote it down, and the New Orleans musicians were first to play the music on other instruments. Certainly ragtime was one of the main ingredients of the New Orleans musical broth. Ragtime made its first appearance at the Chicago World's Fair of 1893. Along with a dancer called Little Egypt and an authentic troupe of musicians from Dahomey, a piano-playing contest was one of the many exotic features of the fair. The piano-playing contest went on for days, attracting a great deal of attention from the public and the press. Several of the contestants played a novel, peppy, rhythmic style that a writer in one of the Chicago newspapers described as "ragged." Somehow the name caught on, and the emerging style came to be known as ragtime. This was in the day when every respectable American home had its own upright piano. Ragtime caught on rapidly. Simplified versions of the complicated virtuoso pieces played by ragtime specialists enjoyed a large sale, and a publishing industry devoted exclusively to ragtime piano compositions appeared in most cities of the East and Midwest.

The centers for serious ragtime playing (and composing) were in Missouri. By 1900 schools of ragtime, led by brilliant performers and supported by composers and publishing houses, were located in Kansas City, St. Louis, and Sedalia. Most of the leading composers and players were black. Ragtime was a written rather than an improvised music, requiring composers with training in harmony and performers with a sound foundation in piano technique, for rags were difficult to play well. Ragtime forms themselves appear to have been derived from brass band music, the most form common being AA BB A CC DD, with a modulation at the halfway point. The harmonies were those heard in the brass band compositions of John Philip Sousa and Arthur Pryor, whose bands—and similar organizations—had conditioned the public's ear to those sounds during several decades of popularity. This sort of material had a strong appeal to musicians in the evolving jazz bands of New Orleans. To the precise format, simple key modulation, familiar harmonies, and strict (2/2) time, jazzmen made their inescapable modifications. As had happened with brass band music, time became free and more flowing, and also more complex; harmonies were "blued" by flatting the third, seventh, and sometimes the fifth scale degrees; and the New Orleans spirit of improvisation soon saw to the creation of polyphonic textures. Among the most popular titles—first appearing in the form of piano ragtime music—to be taken up by New Orleans bands were "Maple Leaf Rag" and "The Entertainer" (Scott Joplin), "Climax Rag" (James Scott), "Sensation Rag" (Joseph Lamb), "Bugle Call Rag" (Eubie Blake), "Twelfth Street Rag" (Euday Bowman), and "Harlem Rag" and "Buffalo Rag" (Tom Turpin).

In the chapter that follows, Pops's discussion of individual jazz styles in New Orleans is extensive and detailed. The musicians he names were founding fathers of styles on cornet, clarinet, trombone, and the instruments of the rhythm section. Louis Armstrong and many others have testified to Joe Oliver's position as the dean of New Orleans cornetists. Sidney Bechet's discography is one of the largest in jazz; Bechet first recorded in 1923 and continued to make records until 1959, the year of his death in France. In the present chronicle Jelly Roll Morton appears as a controversial character, which is the way most jazzmen saw Morton: a man with great talent but a still greater ego, given to endless conversation and boasting. Morton's memoirs, recorded for the Library of Congress by Alan Lomax, remain a prime document of jazz history. Morton's playing, both as a solo pianist and a bandleader, may be heard on several reissues. Tony Jackson did not record. Where available, listening references are furnished in the discography.

—Ross Russell

Chapter 6
Jazzmen

"Drummers are the biggest problem bass players have. It seems like they're always trying to drown out the bass."

When people ask me about who started jazz, I tell them I give the guys in New Orleans the credit for playing it, but the ragtime composers most credit for writing the music. None of the guys who wrote ragtime came from New Orleans. Ragtime music is different from other music because it's a happier kick, and Dixieland is an even happier kick than ragtime. Ragtime is regular 2/4 time and Dixieland is fast 2/4 time, between 2/4 and 3/4 time. What's called jazz today was called ragtime back then, and the blues back then was called honky-tonk music. Bands that played ragtime usually didn't play nothin' else. Some bands you played with you had to play waltzes, schottisches, and polkas, but these were too dicty for the ragtime bands. If you danced to ragtime you could grab the chick and squeeze her any way you wanted to. We played a lot of blues too. Blues were rough and dirty. The blue notes are the strongest notes you can play.

The guys who wrote ragtime for us were Scott Joplin, Tom Turpin, and Walter Jacobs. We should give a lot of credit to St. Louis and Kansas City for those guys. I never met Walter Jacobs; he was in Kansas City and I never was around there much. Tom Turpin was around St. Louis when I was. I was around St. Louis so long a lot of the guys will tell you I'm from there. Tom and his family ran the Jazzland

89

Dance Hall there. I played there a few times with Charlie Creath and Dewey Jackson.

I remember one time Charlie Creath's band played there at a promotion for Jack Johnson, the boxer. Jack, the manager, and his sparring partner were big crooks. They'd put on a thing, collect all the money, and catch the train before they'd pay anybody. I heard about this and told Charlie to get his money early if he wanted to get it. Charlie stayed at the box office and got it as it came in.

Tom Turpin was a cracker—that's what we called a very light-colored person back then. He was thin and about my height. Every once in a while he'd come around where the band was playing with a new number and say, "I'd like you boys to try this." We'd play the tune and he'd get an orchestration of it. He'd thank us and take off. I never knew him to talk much to anyone, but Tom sure wrote some good numbers.

Scott Joplin and Tom Turpin both came from Texas, then worked around Kansas City and St. Louis. Joplin went on to Chicago and then New York. He left St. Louis before I got there.

In order to play Scott Joplin numbers right, you've got to be able to read. A whole lot of the guys back there couldn't read and didn't want to learn. They'd call the guys who could read "cute guys." The bands that couldn't read could play nothing but choruses. They'd play nothing but chorus after chorus.

Jazz is happier music than any other, the beat and the tempo make it. When the white boys started playing it they thought it had to be played fast and loud. Joe Oliver and Manuel Perez used to play together with the Magnolia Band in a little small room and didn't blast anybody out. Nowadays you've got to stand back from the band or get your ears blown out.

For a long time the violin was the top instrument around New Orleans, and then for a while it was the clarinet. Most of the time it was the trumpet. The violin and clarinet could play a whole lot of melody that the trumpet couldn't play. If they don't announce a number that the trumpet plays, you can't tell what it's playing. In all your ragtime bands your trumpet, trombone, and clarinet were your brass, then you had your guitars, drums, and bass for rhythm. The fiddler usually could read and taught the rest of the band the numbers and played a whole lot of everything. That was for a full seven-piece band, and that was a big band. Your brass bands were usually around ten pieces and didn't go over twelve. They played all kinds of dance music. When you got a job with any band around New Orleans, the first thing they put you on was the bass drum for your rhythm. You'd beat that drum, *boom-boom-boom-boom, boom-boom-boom-boom*. It was straight marching band rhythm. Later it changed. The first snare drums I saw in the bands were the bodies of five string banjos. The guys would cut the neck of a banjo, lay it down on a chair, and beat it. They didn't have no stands. The guys liked them because they had a tinny sound. The bass drum had a cymbal on the side to play with the sticks. After a while they had a sock cymbal on the floor that you patted with your foot. Finally they hooked up a hammer to the foot pedal that worked the maul on the bass drum. When you hit the foot pedal, the hammer hit the cymbal and the maul would beat the bass drum.

In the early days when you had a solo, the other instruments were always doing something behind the solo. None of the guys took their horns down for a chorus to let another guy play a solo. When the band knocked off, the whole band romped on a tune from your left hand to your right corner. The music was written so you couldn't take down your horn. You could take your horn down to dry your lip, but you took it right up again. If any of the instruments would quit playing, the manager or whoever hired you would come right over and say, "What's the matter with that guy, is he tired?" or, "Your lip sore, man?" In those days we all sat on stools or chairs so we didn't get so tired of standing like you do today. About 1920 or '21 guys started taking down their horns after they'd blown a chorus. Now the rhythm guys are the only ones who work hard. They play all the way through, and the bass player stands up all the time.

The instrument I've played most is string bass. I also play tuba and a little guitar. I have played cello, but I wasn't so good. The string bass is part of the foundation of a jazz band. It's like a leg on a table. The bass and the drums are the foundation that the rest of the band works on. I don't think the bass or the drums are solo instruments. They're the rhythm, and I don't like to play solos. What I like to do is get to romping on a fast number and slap out a good rhythm.

The bass isn't a loud instrument, but it cuts through the band. It goes *zing, zing,* and just keeps cutting through—you can feel it. When I start playing a number I don't tune up before a number, I wait till the number gets started then I play while I tune when I need.

I don't know who started the pizzicato bass. It was always in music, and I don't think anyone around New Orleans invented it. When we used to pick the bass we'd hold onto the bow at the same time. Now they have little things called bow caddies you put the bow in while you pick. I still usually hold onto the bow while I pick unless I'm going to slap the strings too. In New Orleans we'd have two pick notes in one bar, then you'd go six bars of bowing, and maybe have one note to pick. You can't put your bow down and play that way. In New Orleans we picked two beats to the bar and in New York we started picking four to a bar. Now we pick four or eight beats to a bar or full note.

I first learned to bow the bass, then I started doing a lot of picking. Pretty soon everybody else was picking too, so then I went back to bowing. Before long everybody would be bowing again. It seems like I've been switching like that all my life. I always thought Henry Kimball was the greatest bass player around New Orleans, and he never picked. When he went to work on the boats for the Streckfus people, they told him to go around to me and get some ideas from me. Ever since I'd watched him at Lincoln Park as a kid he was my idol, and I was very embarrassed. My brother Willie told me to go ahead and show him how to pick up on the bass, so I did.

Drummers are the biggest problem bass players have. It seems like they're always trying to drown out the bass by hitting the cymbals. Sometimes they play so loud you can't even hear the trumpet player. In my life I've played with a whole lot of bad drummers and a lot of good ones. Baby Dodds and Tommy Benton are a couple of good ones.

There were two different types of trumpet players in New Orleans. The jazz type played hot and made the band swing. Most of them played like Armstrong, only they started way before him. They had a nice peppery style. They were guys like Joe Oliver, Wild Ned, Buddy Bolden, John Penerton, Buddy Petit, Freddie Keppard, and Louis Armstrong. Their styles were pretty much alike. Then you had the guys that played straight and played more for tone. They were your sweet trumpet players and played real well in a band. The guys in their bands had to put their own swing in the music and make their own feelings. These guys were Bunk Johnson, Papa Celestin, Arnold Metoyer, and Manuel Perez. They really played beautiful tones, but they wouldn't make their own breaks off the melody like the hot trumpet players would. If they had to play a break, it had to be written for them. Bunk would make his own breaks though, even though he was a sweet player.

After the guys from New Orleans got around, guys from the East and West, all of them, tried to play like the guys from New Orleans. A lot of the guys around New Orleans were just loud trumpet players. I think Wild Ned was better than Bolden. Bolden was just a chorus man; he wouldn't play a whole number. Most of the New Orleans bands of the day, you didn't hear them play a full number. The Ory Band and the Eagle Band never played a whole number. "Sweet Georgia Brown," they'd just play the chorus and none of the other part. They never did make no coda; they'd end on the coda and make their own ending.

My favorite trumpet player was Joe Oliver. He played a whole lot of horn. Joe had all kinds of things he put on his horn. He used to shove a kazoo in the bell to give it a different effect. A guy named Tony who played with us in Cairo, Illinois, got a guy to make a thing you put in your horn with two kazoos in it. He had another thing that had about four kazoos welded together that really gave the horn a funny sound. Those babies sold like a house on fire all over the country, and Joe didn't get nothin' for it.

Freddie Keppard and Joe Oliver both used to play with a handkerchief over their fingers. Both of them did it for kicks to bug other guys and didn't do it very much. Sometimes Joe would do it to keep guys from learning a new number we had. We used to have musicians' clubs where you paid 50 cents dues. We'd write away for numbers by Scott Joplin, Tom Turpin, or Walter Jacobs. For a dollar you got four numbers. When we got a number nobody had, we'd cut the title off the sheet and write "Some Stuff" up there and put a number on it to keep track of them. If a guy would ask what it was, we'd say "Some Stuff," and that way he couldn't order a copy of it.

Joe Oliver didn't drink hardly at all; he just chewed a lot of tobacco. He used to get a big pack of stuff they called King Bee Tobacco. He'd hook one finger in the pouch and pull tobacco out—that was one chew. He'd chew it and blow his horn. At the place we were playing there was a hole in the floor where Joe used to spit. He spit there so much it rotted the wood out. He had real bad teeth and pyorrhea that bothered him a lot. Joe was still chewing tobacco when he died. I tried it a few times, but it made me sick.

When we were working the District, Joe and I used to have dinner together almost every night before we went to work. One night I'd buy and next night Joe'd buy. I'd have one hamburger and a glass of milk. Joe would have six hamburgers and a quart of milk, so I always got stung. Back then I had a girl who'd send me some lunch to eat at midnight. Joe and my brother started telling me, "Man, don't eat that stuff, it's poison. Somebody's trying to knock you off, and that food just ain't good for you." Then they'd say it was okay if they ate it because the poison wasn't meant for them. Then Joe and Willie would sit and eat my lunch. I fell for that a long time.

We had a couple of nicknames for Joe. One was "Tenderfoot." He had corns all over his feet and they were always sore. Sometimes they'd get so bad he could hardly walk. He'd buy real big shoes so he'd have lots of room in them. He had a bad temper, and if we wanted to make him mad we'd throw a book down by his feet. He'd jump and really get hot. One night we were playing the Big Easy Hall and Joe got mad at some gal. He threw his trumpet case at her and knocked a big hole in the wall. She said she was gonna go get her gang and clean us out, but she never came back.

Another name we had for Joe was "Chalk" because of his eye. He had a big white spot or growth on his eye, and we called them "chalk eyes." Joe and I were both pool fiends. We used to play a lot to see who could take the money from who. Willie played a lot with us. We'd play straight pool or what you call rotation. The guy who broke usually got all the balls in, and the other guys wouldn't even get a chance to shoot. I was very good until I started wearing glasses way late. Joe didn't talk very much.

Joe and I were always booking dates for each other when we'd play a dance. Up on the stand you were always trying to get dates with the girls for after the dance. Sometimes you'd book three or four girls to wait, and sometimes all of them would wait. Then you'd have to make it out the back window of the dance hall. We'd be up on the stand and Joe would say, "I've got a couple over here," and I'd say, "Man, I've already got two for us over there." It was tough when both of them wanted me or both wanted Joe; we'd have to split them off easy. Back in those days people didn't want their girls hanging out with musicians. They thought we were dirty rats and tramps. Any time you played music you had a bad mark against you. Back then the slick guys would wait until you were making time with some chick, then they'd roll up and say, "Hey, man, how about loaning me a deuce?" They're too embarrassed not to give it to you. It always works. After Joe left New Orleans he started running around with those funny little chicks and spending all his money. When he didn't have no money left, them funny chicks kicked him out.

In New Orleans if you got thrown in jail and you worked you got two days for one. In about 1911 I got sent to jail for 30 days. They claimed I was shooting dice on the street, but I wasn't. I stayed in for two weeks working and having fun. We swept the yard and cleaned up. The guys would sing the blues and keep rhythm with their brooms. The sounds were beautiful. Joe nearly went to jail when we were in the Magnolia Band. All the bands used to wear uniforms. The caps had the name of the band and "Leader" or "Manager" on those guys' hats. The first uniforms we had were green and we wanted some blue ones too. Joe was our treasurer, and he was supposed to order them from Western Uniform Company in Chicago. They cost 12 dollars apiece, which was a whole lot of money then. For about a month there Joe and I went around playing pool, drinking all day, going to baseball games, and having a good time on Joe's money. I didn't know it, but then Joe wrote a letter to the band and had someone mail it from Chicago. It said that the Western Uniform Company had burned down and we couldn't get our uniforms or our money back. The other guys got wise to it and wanted to throw Joe in jail. The Western Uniform Company wanted to furnish the lawyers to get Joe. On one side was Sam Dutrey, Arnold Dupas, Dave Dupas, and Emile Bigard, and on the other was Louis Keppard and I. We said, "We don't want to put Joe in jail, and we won't stand for it." We promised to pay the money back. So I worked driving a cotton wagon for about two months to help Joe pay the money back. Everybody got their money except me. Joe never did pay me and died owing me money. That's why I'd never make records with him.

Buddy Petit was another one of my favorites. He didn't hit a lot of high notes like Armstrong did; he played down in his horn, in the low range. Everything he played was low, nothing way up there and he wasn't any loud trumpet player. He was strictly a jazz player and was very pleasin' to listen to. Buddy couldn't read. A lot of the young guys were like that—they just wouldn't learn. I played with Buddy's band at Spanish Fort in about 1915. Bechet played clarinet with Buddy for a while, and then we had George Boyd. A kid named George Washington played trombone, another kid named Chester played bass for him before I did, Face O [Eddie "Face O" Woods] played drums, and then Chinee Foster did.

Chinee and Buddy used to both stammer. When Chinee would start to say something, Buddy would break in and say, "Aaaw s-s-shut up a-a-a-and let a m-m-m-man what can t-t-t-talk, talk." Chinee also played with Papa Celestin and Jack Carey. George Washington was a little bitty guy; he was shorter than Jimmy Archey. He was in reform school the same time Armstrong was, and he played tuba in the reform school band with Louis. One night we were playing and this real ugly guy with one eye and big red lips came up to George Boyd and said, "My word and honor George, you're an ugly man." The whole band cracked up, and we couldn't play for laughin'. George was ugly, but the guy who told him was twice as ugly.

Buddy and I used to get limber drunk on the bandstand. We couldn't even stand up. Buddy drank more than I did, and he'd get so drunk we'd have to tie him down to keep him from knockin' himself out. I don't remember him getting into any trouble except for hurtin' himself. Buddy was drunk all the time, and he finally drank himself to death.

Buddy's father or stepfather, I don't know what he really was, was Joe Petit. Joe only had one tooth in his mouth but he played the loudest valve trombone you wanted to hear. I don't know how he did it. Joe had a horse that got sick and laid down next to their house. The horse started kicking around and got under the house, then he died and after a few hours started to swell up. He raised the whole house up and they couldn't get him out. Finally they called the aggravatin' wagon to come and pull him out. You had to pay two dollars to have them come and haul a horse or mule away. Big Eye Louis was Buddy's cousin.

Two other jazz trumpet players I liked were Joe Johnson and Louis Armstrong. Louis and I used to drive coal wagons around New Orleans. I worked for Pittsburgh Coal and he worked for Tennessee Coal. Every morning we used to meet at a joint and have some whiskey. One morning I'd buy and the next he'd buy. When Louis was playing at Tom Anderson's with my brother, Willie would play the tunes on the violin so Louis and Albert Nicholas could get them down. In all Louis's books and things he never mentions Willie. Willie could read very good and play any stringed instrument. He taught me more about playing the bass than anybody, and he played with most of the good bands around New Orleans. Louis should've given him credit for the things he taught him. Kid Shots Madison and Kid Rena were high-range jazz trumpet players like Louis was.

Manuel Perez was a wonderful trumpet player and a nice guy. He was one of the best. Manuel and Joe Oliver were working in a 13-piece brass band for a while, and you could hear those two trumpets over all that other noise. Both of them were very powerful guys. Manuel and all those Creole guys were carpenters and cigar makers. If you needed a house built, a gang of them would get together and build you a nice four-room house in a day. They'd play music, drink wine and beer, have gumbo and sandwiches, and have a picnic building a house for you.

Louis DuMaine fooled around with the trumpet a long time before anyone would hire him. He played sweet and could read more than most young trumpet players we had down there. He was good and wasn't no loud trumpet player. I got him to come on the boats with us. He made one trip and got sick. He stayed sick for a long time. People loved his playing but he was too sickly to stay. Years ago the doctors never knew what you had; they just took your money and that was it. Sometimes you'd get well and sometimes you'd go the way of Fat Henry. That means you quit the scene or died.

Frank Keeley was a very good trumpet player. He was one of the first guys to leave for Chicago. That was about 1907 before Sugar Johnny, who went in about 1908, and Freddie Keppard, who went in 1909. Frank would come to New Orleans and stay awhile after that and then go to Chicago for a while. When Freddie left he had a lot of jobs lined up, and somebody would get a group to play them. The last job I played with Frank was a pickup group we'd gotten together to handle a job Freddie had gotten playing a picnic at the lake. Frank was a bad kind of guy, rough and hard to get along with. He used to make all kinds of funny sounds on his horn; one was making it sound like a chicken. Joe Johnson used to do that too. The last time I saw Frank was in Henry Martin's barbershop in New Orleans about 1926 or 1927. Henry was a drummer. His shop was on Custom House between Franklin and Basin. That's where the sporting-house cribs were, and after they ran the girls out the cribs made nice barbershops.

Amos Riley was a violin player first, then he started playing trumpet. He had his own little band. It was one of the uptown bands. Amos was a nice little trumpet player but not too good. My brother was with them for a while. Alec Smith played string bass. He also played some guitar, and he was one of the guys who taught me some things about string bass. Amos also played with the Silver Leaf Band and the Gold Leaf Band around the Irish Channel. Albert Baptiste was leader of the Silver Leaf Band. I played with both of these bands around 1910, 1911, and 1912, but they didn't get much work. Another trumpet player who used to play the big dances with the Silver and Gold Leaf bands was George McCullun. He was a nice trumpet player and worked as a cotton grader. He also played with Robichaux's band. His son was named George, and he played trumpet and was a cotton grader too.

Another Uptown band was the Primrose Band that was led by Hamp Benson, the trombone player. Joe Johnson was their trumpet player when he first started out. It was a reading band. One night Hamp collected the money that was due the band and they never saw him again. About 15 years later, about 1925, I saw him in St. Louis. That was the only trouble I knew of around New Orleans of the leader paying you off. You sure had trouble with the guy who put on the dance or party, but you never had any trouble with the bandleader.

Willie Hightower was a trumpet player who had a little band that played St. Catherine's Hall on Saturday nights. Willie was a real nice guy, but he didn't play enough horn for me. There were quite a few nice guys around New Orleans who didn't play much horn. I had worked with Joe Oliver, Freddie Keppard, Manuel Perez, John Penerton, and guys like Hightower weren't high-powered like they were. Willie had Baby Dodds on drums and Roy Palmer on trombone, and I can't remember the rest of the guys' names. Roy went from guitar to trumpet to trombone to baritone horn. He was playing the baritone the last time I saw him in Chicago. Hightower was a carpenter for his regular job. Dave Perkins taught him the trumpet, and Dave taught most of the guys around there. Willie left New Orleans about 1914 or 1915 for Chicago.

Tig Chambers was a cornet player and a barber that had a little band. Little James Williams was his clarinet player. His father, James Williams, played trumpet with Robichaux's band for a long time. Little James came out here to California and died out here. Yank Johnson played valve trombone—his brother Buddy played trombone in the Superior Band—a guy named Nini was on drums; Pete Dutrey on violin; Emmett Johns was the guitar player. Johns went to Chicago and quit music to run a kotch game [a card game]. He played string bass too. Another guy we got was Willie Humphrey on clarinet after Little James left for California. I played with Tig's band in about 1919 and was with them for a pretty good while. We used to work the Willow Lawn every Monday night; it was at Josephine and Willow. One night Tig made me mad, and I walked off the job on them and never came back.

There was one guy named Thornton Blue who played real good trumpet, and I played in his band around 1912 or 1913. We mostly rehearsed and didn't have no job. I also worked with him driving cotton wagons for Grants. Blue used to play very loud, and at a funeral one day he was blowin' so hard he just dropped dead. He lived out in the Irish Channel and had his own little band. Kaiser Josephs played clarinet, Face O was the drummer, and Oscar Kendalls the bass player. Their trombone player was named Black Joe. He hit those screaming notes like Armstrong did on trumpet. For a while he had New Orleans all sewed up—no one could hit those notes but him. That's all he could play though, he didn't know nothing about music. He had to slur his horn up to a note like Ory, but he could play with any band that way. He also played with Kid Rena, Tig Chambers, and some of the other small groups around town.

One of the reasons it's hard to remember a lot of the guys who played is there aren't too many pictures of them. A lot of the guys didn't want any pictures of them made. They said it was a jinx.

Jack Carey played trombone and got the Jack Carey Crescent Band together. Jack was a guy who had kids all around New Orleans. We'd be playing a place and someone would come around saying one of Jack's kids had died. Sometimes we'd play two or three funerals and find out they were all for Jack's kids. I played with Jack's band in about 1914 and 1915. In Jack's band we had an old guy named George Caldwell who played clarinet. He used to carry three clarinets on a job with him, a C, B, and A. Some nights I'd unscrew all the clarinet parts and put them back together wrong. He'd spend the whole night trying to get them together right, and he'd be a hot baby. Another clarinet player we had was Willie Humphrey. His father, Jim Humphrey, played trumpet and couldn't stand me. He was always saying, "You'll never be a musician," and "You'll never play nothin'." We'd be playing someplace and he'd start worryin' me with "You'd better learn how to read." I'd say, "Oh, man, go hide yourself," or "Don't rush yourself, go ahead and play." Those old guys wanted to read and play different than we did. Jim Humphrey and John Robichaux wanted to play one way, and Freddie Keppard and us wanted to play ragtime. Old man Humphrey didn't like anybody who couldn't read, and he didn't like the way I picked the bass—he wanted me to bow it. His son Willie came to L.A. and played tenor sax around L.A. with Mutt Carey for 20 years. Willie had a son named Little Willie Humphrey that played clarinet too. I played with him on the boats with Dewey Jackson. Jack Carey's band was out at the lake playing a picnic one Sunday. Everybody had brought a big picnic basket and put them up on the bandstand, then went to stroll around. Jack started snooping around through the baskets tasting the wine. He reached over a mud puddle to get one bottle and fell in with his white suit on. After we quit laughing, we went off and stole a tablecloth and wrapped him up in it. He played all afternoon standing up there wrapped in that tablecloth.

George Filhe was the best trombone player around New Orleans. He worked in the early Imperial Band. George was great, very musical. He knew his horn and could hit a note; he didn't have to look around for it. Another very good trombone player was a guy we called Sugah. He played with Edward Clem's band, and they mostly played the Funky Butt Hall at Liberty and Franklin.

Willie Santiago was a good guitar player when he wasn't sleeping. He'd sleep on the bandstand all night long, then when we got off he'd want to shadowbox and horse around. There was a beer and wine place called the Alley that Willie hung out at. If we needed him for a job we'd go there and get him. He played with a lot of different bands and was with the Olympic Band for awhile.

Big Eye Louis Nelson was the best ragtime clarinet player we had down there. He was strictly a jazz clarinet player. He didn't know as much music as the other guys like Picou, George Baquet, Charlie McCurdy, Sam Dutrey, and those guys who were straight clarinet players. Louis always played a C clarinet and played the violin parts. Albert Nicholas was almost as good as Louis, but he wasn't as fast and he never could read too good. Albert was very hard to get along with; he had his own ways and he didn't want nobody to tell him nothing. His uncle, Wooden Joe, played a beautiful trumpet. Johnny Dodds was very good on the stuff he knew. But Big Eye Louis played hot and played more clarinet than anybody in those days. I really liked to play with him because he had such a nice style. Big Eye Louis was the greatest clarinet player I ever played with.

Next to Big Eye Louis, Sidney Bechet played the most jazz clarinet around New Orleans. I started playing with Sidney when we were both kids and both of us played in the Jack Carey Band for a long time. I'm six years older than him. Sidney played in the District with Jack Carey. He was an ear musician and a wonderful jazzman. One night we ended up in jail together. He was fooling around with a chick at a dance out at the lake. She pulled a knife and stabbed him. I grabbed a stick and started after her. When the cops came we told them we were playing. They took us to jail and then let us go. When we got back to the dance, she thanked us for not getting her in trouble. Sidney was always wanting to fight, but they never did come off. Sidney is all for himself and jealous of everyone. He and Louis Armstrong were two of a kind—you didn't make any showing when you played with them. I played with Sidney all of my life and I used to tell him, "Your name is in the lights, man, nobody can hurt you. If you've got a good band with you, it makes you better." But he wouldn't listen. Sidney could play a little on almost any instrument and could pick some guitar.

Sidney wasn't the only guy who got into trouble. Black Benny, the drummer, was always in trouble and lived in jail most of the time. He was a very good bass drummer, and when we had a funeral to play we'd go down to the captain and get him to let Benny out of jail to play. Then after we'd take him back to jail. His house was only about four blocks from the jail. When he did something wrong, the police would send some kid down to tell him to come in, and he'd come. Once Benny got a new serge suit and was wearin' it when a policeman picked him up and handcuffed him. He told the cop he was gonna wear the suit that day and he'd go to jail the next day. The cop wouldn't let him go, so he got mad and started runnin' while he was still handcuffed. He drug the policeman through the mud in the streets and tore his new serge suit. Afterward he said he was sorry. Benny was a mean ignorant guy—he'd hit a woman with a piece of wood or a bat or anything and knock her down. That's how he got killed. He hit this woman and then turned his back on her and she cut him down.

Jean Vigne, the drummer, had kids all over the country. Wherever we'd land, he'd have a kid there. We couldn't go anyplace he didn't have a kid. Jean had a funny color; you couldn't tell what he was. He was light brown with straight hair. His wife was very light too. One night we were playing the Come Clean Hall over in Gretna, and before we started I asked Jean, "Hey, you got any kids over here?"

He said, "No man, it's not like that."

After a while the doorman come up to him and said, "Mr. Vigne, somebody wants to see you at the door. He says he's your kid."

Jean jumped off the stand, went and got him, and introduced him around. Afterward I said, "How many more you got over here, Jean?" He said, "Oh, man, I don't know," in that fine voice of his.

Jean had a business in the District selling bundles of wood and little buckets of coal to the girls so they could keep warm while they stood in their doorways and hustled tricks. He was partners with MacMurray, who was another good drummer. He could read like [Louis] Cottrell and was more of a show drummer. Jean must have had a million kids; it seems like everywhere we played a funeral some kid was coming up calling him Daddy. One of his boys, Sidney Vigne, was a wonderful saxophone player, and he had a band on the boats for a while. Another of his kids I got to know was Babe. He was a sweet-back boy who hung around with all the musicians a lot but never played nothing.

Lorenzo Stall the guitar player was another guy like Jean. When us musicians would go out in the country towns we'd always make out. Lorenzo was so popular he'd have girls waiting outside his room for their turn to go in. He was very good looking. Lorenzo played mostly guitar and was good; he played some banjo later on. He was with the Jack Carey Band and Ory's band. He ran a little pressing shop and had a couple of girls on the line for him all the time. When he died I was with the Gold Whispering Band. Our whole band went and marched behind him.

The first slide trombone I ever saw was brought down to New Orleans by a cousin of mine, George Williams. That was right around the time we left the plantation. George had gone up to Memphis and gotten a job with W.C. Handy's band. He got the slide trombone there and brought it back with him on a visit. Up until then there was nothing but valve trombones. The whole town was excited about them, and guys started buying them. There were a whole bunch of numbers you could play on them. The minstrel shows started using them a whole lot too. At first the guys who bought slide trombones would bring the valve and slide trombone on jobs. They'd use the slide on numbers like "Slidin' Jim." Now you hardly see anything but slide trombones.

Before W.C. Handy went to Chicago and then New York, where I got to know him, he had a band in Memphis. It traveled all down through the South, and it played mostly society dates. The band was called a blues band, but they didn't really play any blues. They just played everything straight. It sure wasn't a jazz band. In a jazz band you play a chorus as an introduction so you'll know what they're play- ing, then they take off. With him it all came out like it was written in the book. His band was a society band like Robichaux's.

I got to know Handy pretty well up around New York. He had a store that was just one big room where you could sit around. He sold copies of his tunes there, and he published a couple of numbers for other guys. I made some records with him around 1938 or 1939, and I used to go down to his store sometimes to try and teach his son to play the vibraphones. His son had a very fine set of vibraphones, but he never did learn to play them.

Old man Handy was a nice old guy, and he got all his fame from writing the "St. Louis Blues." He actually stole it from a guy named Frank Butts who was a honky-tonk player around Memphis. Butts called it "I Got the Mojo Blues."

Handy was supposed to get the tune copyrighted for Butts, but he changed the name to "St. Louis Blues" and copyrighted it for himself. Jelly knew all about the deal, and every time Jelly would see Handy talking on a corner to some guys, he would get on the other corner and start telling guys all about Butts and Handy as loud as he could so Handy could hear. I never knew Butts, but Jelly claimed he knew all about what happened, and he used to cuss Handy out and call him a "horse thief."

The Boston Symphony made the "St. Louis Blues" for Handy by playing it and making it popular. The rich people around New York knew about it and Handy, and they used to hire him for society dates. Once you've heard the "St. Louis Blues" you've also heard the "Memphis Blues" and the "Beale Street Blues"—they're all the same. If you're playing any of those tunes you've really got to watch yourself that you don't play the wrong tune, they're so close. Handy never claimed he was any "Father of the Blues" around me or any of the colored—we knew he wasn't.

These tonks like Butts played in were really something to see. Most of them were for the roustabouts who worked on the levees. They had them in St. Louis, Kansas City, Memphis, New Orleans, and a lot of other places. Tonks had piano playing, drinking, and gambling. There was always a pool table or two in a tonk, but the guys never played no pool. They'd block the pockets up and use it for shootin' craps. When the cops would come around to check you out, everybody would throw the balls on the table, unstop the pockets, and get the cue sticks down. The cops would come in, look around, and see a nice little pool game goin. As soon as they'd take off the crap game would get goin' again. Those guys were so well organized it was really something funny to see.

All around the New Orleans area we had street-corner players. They used guitar and mandolin and played for coins on the corners. If they did pretty good they'd enlarge and add string bass. Those guys would walk down the street, and when they'd see a gang of people they'd stop and play them a number. Then they'd pass the hat around. Guys would put a coin in. Lonnie Johnson and his daddy and his brother used to go all over New Orleans playing on street corners. Lonnie played guitar, and his daddy and brother played violin. Lonnie was the only guy we had around New Orleans who could play jazz guitar. He was great on guitar. Django Reinhardt was a great jazz player like Johnson. They'd really take off on a number. Lonnie was tough to follow.

There were a lot of blind and crippled street musicians in the South, but the only one I remember around New Orleans was Blind Freddie. He was born blind and played a whole lot of harmonica in the streets. One day he put down his harmonica and the next day he was playing clarinet. For a while there he played with a lot of bands. Then he got some kind of religion and quit playing. After that he told fortunes for a long time. He could tell your voice and name you no matter how long it had been since he saw you last.

Most of the street corner players came out of the woods or some little town someplace.

A lot of times in New Orleans I used to take my bass and walk down the streets of the District in the daytime looking for someone to invite me to play. I'd pass a whorehouse and tonk, and one of the piano players would yell, "Hey George, come on in and play something." We'd play a few numbers, have a couple of drinks, and I'd move on. I never played with a band in a whorehouse, because they don't hire bands. All the piano players played in theaters, tonks, or whorehouses. The only bands who had piano players were Robichaux and the Tuxedo Band.

Every whorehouse had piano players, but Lulu White's had the most. If you needed an extra piano player, you called Lulu's and they'd send you one. Lulu's place was the biggest and highest-class sporting house in New Orleans. Today they call Lulu White's place Mahogany Hall but we never did. You went in there and she asked you what you wanted. She had any color, nationality, kinky hair, straight hair, blond, or almost anything you wanted. Lulu had different prices for different girls and different rooms and according to how long you wanted to stay and what you wanted to do. She had beds where the headboards and footboards were mirrors and you could watch yourself while you were doing it. There weren't any 50-cent or one-dollar girls at Lulu's; they were 25 dollars or 50 dollars depending on what you wanted.

Lulu White herself could handle three men at once—one in every hole. She called that her "around the world trip." That was very expensive. Lulu herself liked women for sex.

I never got to play with Jelly Roll Morton around New Orleans and didn't get to know him real well until we were in New York. Around New Orleans sometimes I used to let him take me to some of the whorehouses with him. He'd take me in, talk big, and show me some of his chicks. He was very flashy; he'd get four or five one-dollar bills and wrap them around a roll of silk paper to make it look like he had a roll. A lot of the guys used to do that. Jelly worked mostly at Lulu White's place, and back then was just another piano player who worked the District.

The Twenty-five Club was open twenty-four hours, and most of the piano players who played the District used to come there before and after work. Jelly never did come around the Twenty-five Club or hang out with the musicians around New Orleans. Jelly knew more of the guys after he left New Orleans than he did when he was there, and he never played in a band until he went to Chicago. Jelly actually was from around Biloxi or Bay St. Louis, Mississippi. That's where his mother and her people are from. He talked a lot about fighters and cabarets and all that stuff that none of the guys knew anything about. All the young kids up in New York used to listen to Jelly talk, and they believed him. He just blasted away, and they got a lot of publicity for him he really didn't deserve. I knew Jack the Bear he talked about. She was a bad woman and lived on Julie Drive. She wasn't as bad as some of the guys. Aaron and Boar Hog were the two baddest guys down there. They weren't bad to everybody, just to little weak and lame guys. They'd catch a lame guy and beat him up. Musicians always thought they were tough and could fight, but they couldn't. Guys like Aaron and Boar Hog would beat them up when they caught them.

Jelly was what we called a big-time pimp around New Orleans. He had that gold on his teeth and a diamond in one. If you wanted to find Jelly you had to go to the whorehouses, because that's where he'd be pimpin'. Music was just a sideline for him to prove he had something to work at in the District. If Jelly wasn't in a whorehouse he was trying to be a slick pool shooter or a card shark. He wanted everybody to think he was a big-time gambler, but he couldn't shoot pool and wasn't a very good gambler. If you listened to Jelly talk about gambling, you'd think he was the greatest gambler in the world, but if you played with him you'd know different. Just like he did a lot of lying on his [Library of] Congress records. He claimed he invented a lot of things he didn't. If you'd listen to him talk long enough, he'd claim he invented the piano or anything else that came to his mind. When he'd get through talking, he'd make you believe anything he told you; he was a very good talker. Jelly was always talking himself into something. I'm only speaking facts about Jelly, because he's still a friend of mine.

Jelly had a nice style of playing the backward bass. A whole lot of guys play that style now. He had a lot of numbers he could play, like "The Pearls." He worked both of his hands together; he couldn't work one separate from the other. He had a good right hand, but his left hand was no good. If you listen to "The Pearls" and "King Porter Stomp," you can tell how them hands worked together. "King Porter Stomp" is strictly a bass number, and Jelly had to get someone else to play it right for him. I don't know this first-hand, but some of the guys said that he had to get high-powered guys like Tony Jackson, Albert Carroll, or Udell Wilson to go and cut the bass parts of a record for him. Jelly would play the melody with his right hand and the other guy would play the bass behind what he did. It was like Pete Johnson, Meade Lux Lewis, and Albert Ammons. Pete played more blues than any of them, and Meade Lux Lewis played a lot of blues, but they didn't have no left hand and could only play in one key. Albert Ammons was a musician who could play with both hands in any key. Albert would play the bass parts for them on records. Pete and Meade Lux Lewis could never play in any band because of just playing in one key. Jelly is what we called a honky-tonk piano player.

Jelly was the best-entertaining piano player by himself in the sporting houses. He knew all the dirty songs, and that's where he was great. When a customer would come in the door, Jelly would make up a dirty rhyme on your name and play it to his piano playing. Even if you'd walk by the place, he'd get off a rhyme and start vamping on the piano. They didn't play or sing no pop numbers. We had another guy around New Orleans named Black Pete that was great at that too. A bass player named George Jones was the best at rhymes. He made more money than any musician around New Orleans and couldn't play a nickel's worth of bass. He worked the whorehouses, banquets, and parties. Everybody would hire him. If you were giving a party, you'd hire him and give him a list of the names of the people who were coming. When they'd walk in, he'd saw on his bass and make up a funny rhyme on their name. After the guests were there, he'd stand up sawing the bass and talking funny. He even had a special pocket he kept most of his tips in. Sometimes during the party he'd turn his pockets out to show how little money he'd made, and people would give him more. Jelly did rhyming like George except Jelly put more music to it.

Jelly was right that the piano players in those days made more money than other musicians. They got a lot of tips because they were playing the whorehouses. Jelly also got in ASCAP before any of the other musicians from New Orleans and claimed all kinds of blues numbers. Before that they were anybody's numbers. They were just blues in B-flat or some other key. He used to play the numbers and have a writer there to write the notes down. Then they'd make up a lead sheet, send it in, and get it copyrighted.

Up in New York I used to play with Jelly. I never used to sit around and listen to him play and talk, though. He was always talking one thing and doing another. He said that jazz music should be played softly with plenty of swing. But Jelly didn't play what he talked; he talked sweet jazz and played a juggy style. It didn't swing like most jazz and wasn't up-to-date like James P. Johnson's.

Around New York, Jelly would always be saying he had a job and start getting a band together for rehearsal. He'd hire a rehearsal hall, and we'd rehearse with him for two or three weeks, then nothing would happen. What would happen was Jelly had a job all right. He'd talk himself on a job, but he'd just keep talking to the guy who was going to hire him, and before he'd get to play, he'd talk himself right out. The guy would fire Jelly just so he wouldn't have to listen to him talk. He got a job playing the World's Fair in 1932, that I was gonna be on. We got fired before we opened up, but we got a week's pay and didn't do no work. Jelly told us the guy was scared for his money and got salty. Most of the time we didn't get any pay, but we'd be glad to come to rehearsal because we didn't have no job anyhow. I don't think Jelly really cared whether he got the job or not because he had plenty of money coming in from song royalties.

Jelly couldn't play good behind someone's singing. There's a whole lot of piano players who can't do that. Earl Hines, as great as he is, can't play with a singer. Guys like Jelly and Hines are too much for themselves—they're so busy playing for themselves you can't hear the singer for what the piano player's doing. Jelly was a good man by himself or in one of those whorehouses.

One time in New York we made some records with Wilton Crawley. Crawley hired Jelly to get a group together for the date, then he forgot about it. He hired Luis Russell to get another group together for the same date. Both groups showed up for the date. Jelly was really hot—him and Crawley spent the whole two hours for the date arguing. We had to come back for the next day to make the records. Jelly and the Victor people told Crawley he had to pay all the musicians. So Crawley had to pay for three groups, two the first day and one the second. Jelly came back and played the piano with us.

The most harm Jelly ever did was to himself. He just talked too much. Musicians called him "Loudmouth" or "Run at the Mouth." He'd stand on a corner and talk very loud and get himself in trouble. He used to always tell me that New Orleans had the best musicians. I'd argue with him and say, "No, man, New Orleans had the luckiest musicians. You take Johnny Dodds, Sidney Bechet, and those guys, they just lucked up on making some early records. Guys like Manuel Perez, Arnold Metoyer, Frank Keeley, and Tig Chambers, they could play, but where are they?" I think there were a lot of guys around New Orleans and New York like James P. Johnson who played better than Jelly.

One piano player Jelly talked about that was a great piano player was Tony Jackson. He wrote some good music too. He didn't play flashy like Jelly, but what he did, he did nice. His stuff had more swing than Jelly, but even Clarence Williams had more swing than Jelly. Tony and Clarence wrote down a lot of tunes for Jelly, and Clarence might have stolen some from Jelly; Clarence was a horse thief.

Tony was one of the first guys to leave for Chicago. He left about the time Frank Keeley did. All of those guys took the train. A lot of little trumpet players went up. Sugar Johnny went up. He had a trumpet style like Armstrong and Oliver. He was a huge guy, bigger than Keppard or Oliver. I think he was from around Breakaway, Louisiana. He played at Pete Lala's for a long time before he left. Another guy who left early was a guy named "Pork." He played for a while and finally got on the Chicago police force. He was a chief detective and played in the policemen's band. When Joe Oliver went up, he made it bigger than any of them because he started to make records.

There were a lot of piano players around New Orleans besides Jelly. Some of them were Alfred Wilson, Sore Dick, Albert Calb, Drag Nasty, Udell Wilson, Clarence Williams, Black Pete, and a whole bunch of guys. Udell Wilson was from Kansas City, and a lot of the guys came from places like that to get jobs working the District. Black Pete played at a small house on Gaspar Street. Albert Carroll used to play out at the theater in Lincoln Park.

The piano players waited for their tricks just like the girls did. If a trick was good for the girls, it was good for the piano player too. Most of the guys who went in the whorehouses were half stewed and the drunker they were, the more money they'd tip. The customer picked out the girl and piano player he wanted, and they'd go off to a room. The customer and the girl would drink and make love while the piano player would play some slow blues. The piano players only made 50 cents or one dollar a night from the house, but sometimes they'd made 50 dollars or 60 dollars a night in tips. They never wanted to see a guy come in with a tuxedo on, because they knew they didn't have nothin' in their pockets and they wouldn't get a good tip.

Most of the guys who played piano around New Orleans wouldn't play with a band. We'd call them sissies or say, "Look at that faggot up there." The band musicians thought piano was for women. The guys who played piano would learn another instrument like guitar or violin to get with a band. The guitar was the piano for the bands. There were other reasons we didn't use a piano. The band had to bring the instruments, and you can't carry no piano around with you, and none of the places had pianos in them. Another reason was most of the piano players couldn't read and could only play in one key like F-sharp. Most of the bands couldn't transpose the music to play with them.

A couple of guys I remember who switched instruments to play in a band were Tommy Benton and a guy named Cato. Cato had a stiff leg, so we called him "Pineleg." He learned to play string bass; Tommy learned to play guitar. He said he didn't want no one calling him a sissy and all that. If we were at a place where they had a piano, Tommy would play it sometimes. He couldn't read music but could play in all the keys.

The Tuxedo Band was the first band after Robichaux's to use piano. They had to rent their own piano and put it in the dance hall. A guy named [Richard M.] My Knee Jones played the piano for them. I called him "Pineleg," and for a long time I thought he had a wooden leg, but it was just stiff and didn't have any feeling in it. When I played with the band I used to hit his leg with my bow and say, "I just wanted to see if you're in tune with us." He published a couple of numbers around New Orleans.

Steve Lewis, the piano player who played with Piron, lived next door to me when we were kids. He lived with his aunt, and she didn't want him to play piano. When she'd go off she'd lock him out of the house so he couldn't play the piano. He'd wait until she was gone, then climb in a window to practice. I'd watch for him, and if she'd come too soon, I'd throw some rocks at the house so he could get in before she caught him. Steve couldn't read, but Piron taught him to play in all the keys.

Clarence Williams was a friend of mine in New Orleans. He worked some in the sporting houses, but not as much as the other guys. Clarence knew Jelly in New Orleans, but I don't think Jelly taught him any piano. Clarence knew how to play piano before he left Plaquemine, Louisiana. I don't think Jelly could teach anybody anything because he was too busy talking.

Clarence wasn't down there too long when he and Armand Piron opened a little music store and music publishing house. I think that was around 1910 or 1912. We used to rehearse there sometimes. If you had written a number, you'd go to Clarence to write it down. He could write very fast; as fast as you could do the number, he could write it down. After he'd write it down, he'd arrange it and send it to have it copyrighted and published. Clarence always managed to cut himself in on a number. When a number was published, it would have four or five names on it. Clarence would get as much of it as he could. His name would be in two or three places, and the guy who really wrote it was usually way down the line. After he got through, he had more of your number than you did. Louis Armstrong wrote "Sister Kate" and had Clarence put it down, copyrighted and published it, and Louis never did get nothin' for it. Clarence was a real horse thief. We called him "Spool Head." He didn't have that little old sharp head for nothin'. None of us ever called him "Spool Head" to his face though. Around New Orleans I didn't know Clarence was my cousin. I found that out way late in New York.

Clarence was the first guy from New Orleans to go up North and start making records. He played piano on a whole lot of them. It was really something to make records in those days. They had a megaphone for everyone to play in, and they couldn't record certain instruments, like the string bass. If you cut a hog [made a mistake] in a record in those days, you had to stop and start over on a whole new wax. Sometimes you even had to come back later and do it all over. Nowadays if you cut a hog, they have you play a couple of bars over and splice it in.

The shuttering of Storyville put more prostitutes than jazz musicians on the rolls of the unemployed, but for the latter there was sufficient belt tightening. Some of the steadiest jobs had gone, and New Orleans musicians began to pay attention to reports filtering back from Chicago about high wages there and the brisk demand for those who could play in the authentic style that seemed a New Orleans monopoly. Public interest in the new musical style had been whetted by appearances of the Original Dixieland Jazz Band and by their fast-selling records on the Victor label. By 1920 Freddie Keppard, King Oliver, Johnny and Baby Dodds, Sidney Bechet, Honoré Dutrey, and Emanuel Perez were in Chicago. Others, like Jelly Roll Morton, Papa Mutt Carey, and Kid Ory, went to California. Still others, Pops among them, took employment on the riverboats; they too were headed north, though at a more leisurely pace. Pops Foster began his travels in 1917 when he joined the Fate Marable Jazz Syncopators on the SS Belle of the Bend. Marable was a leading contractor of bands for riverboats. A pianist and steam calliope virtuoso, Marable was a native of Paducah, Kentucky, who had been employed on riverboats almost continuously after 1907. Alumni of Fate Marable bands would eventually include Pops, Louis Armstrong, Red Allen, the Dodd brothers, Emanuel Perez, Johnny St. Cyr, and, later, Al Morgan, Earl Bostic, Gene Sedric, and Jimmy Blanton, Duke Ellington's great bass player. Marable remained on the riverboats until they stopped using bands in the '30s and then worked ashore in St. Louis, where he died in 1947.

The riverboats were floating dance halls, the natural successors to the romantic sidewheelers eulogized by Mark Twain in Life on the Mississippi and to the showboats that brought opera and minstrelry to the river towns at the turn of the century. Since few towns boasted ballrooms, what could have been more convenient than to bring both dance hall and an authentic New Orleans orchestra to the town dock for an afternoon or evening of fun? The Belle of the Bend belonged to a fleet of riverboats operated by the Streckfus family of New Orleans, pioneers of the floating dance hall idea. Musicians ate, slept, lived, and played together aboard ship for weeks or months at a stretch. Bandleaders, usually older than the sidemen, acted as heads of their musical families. Discipline was strict; drunkards and agitators were weeded out and discharged along the way. Most veterans of the riverboats have described the food and accommodations as good; in addition to one's keep, the salaries, although not princely, afforded the more provident an opportunity to accumulate a stake. The riverboats ran as far north as St. Paul; occasionally they found their way up the Missouri and Ohio rivers. In this fashion New Orleans jazz spread through Middle America. The towns where the boats stopped made significant contributions to jazz style in the following generations. Bix Beiderbecke lost no opportunity to hear the floating orchestras when they played his hometown of Davenport, Iowa. St. Louis was much impressed by New Orleans trumpet stars Keppard, Armstrong, and Oliver, and ended up becoming a trumpet-player's town and the center of a school of brilliant brass style beginning with Dewey Jackson and ending with Miles Davis.

Two photographs show Pops Foster during his riverboat period. One shows the Fate Marable band on the SS Sidney with Baby Dodds, drums; Bebe Ridgley, trombone; Joe Howard and Louis Armstrong, cornets; Fate Marable, piano; David Jones, alto horn; Johnny Dodds, clarinet; Johnny St. Cry, banjo; and Foster, string bass. The photograph is dated 1918. The other, taken in the early '20s, shows Eddie Allen's Gold Whispering Orchestra aboard the SS Capitol, another Streckfus boat, with Johnny St. Cyr on banjo and Pops on tuba and doubling on bass. As Pops has told us, he played both instruments, and from his account and that of other jazzmen it is evident that a great deal of doubling took place. The role of the contrabass as the essential string instrument of the jazz rhythm section was not firmly established until the late '20s.

—Ross Russell

Chapter 7
On the Boats

"Most everybody came alone but left with somebody on their arm....everybody was having fun in those days."

❧

From about 1915 to 1917 I was with Armand Piron's orchestra at Tranchina's. At first we had Arthur Campbell on piano, Peter Bocage on trumpet, Tom Benton on guitar, me on bass, and Piron, violin. Arthur Campbell left after a while and Tom Benton took over on piano, and then Johnny St. Cyr took his place on guitar. About this time piano started being used in some places. Usually we didn't have a trombone, but once in a while we did. Spanish Fort was like Coney Island; it was on the lake. They had a mean chef out at Tranchina's, a real nasty guy. He was supposed to feed us a steak dinner one night and he wouldn't, so Johnny St. Cyr and me quit. When they got it straightened out, I had gone to longshore work that paid more money.

About a week after I quit at Tranchina's, Captain Johnny Streckfus and Peter Bocage came for me to go on the boats. They had Frankie Dusen's Eagle Band out there for a while, but they couldn't make it because they had to read music and they couldn't. Most of the big stars around New Orleans couldn't read. It was the first time colored musicians had ever worked on the boats. For about two months we rounded up musicians for the Streckfus people. We couldn't get Baby Dodds right away, so we got another guy named Alexander Lewis. He was a nice little drummer. He didn't think the job was gonna last, so he quit and went with one of them little touring shows. We had Louis Cottrell for a while. He was one of the best drummers we had around New Orleans both for a show drummer and an all-around drummer. Any music you gave him he could play. We ended up having three or four drummers before we finally got Baby Dodds, who could read good enough. I went down to St. Catherine's Hall where he was playing every Sunday night with Willie Hightower's band and finally got him to come with us. Everybody was crazy about him.

Joe Howard and Peter Bocage played trumpets in the band. Peter could also play violin and trombone; he was good. We got Sam Dutrey on clarinet; Dave Jones on mellophone; Johnny St. Cyr, banjo; Frankie Dusen, trombone; Fate Marable on piano; Baby Dodds on drums; and me on bass. When the picture was taken on the boat, Sam Dutrey was drunk that day so Johnny Dodds came and sat in for him. Frankie Dusen was on and off the boats twice; he just couldn't read and we got Babe Ridgley. Fate had been on the boat a long time playing at the piano bar at the back of the boat. A lot of guys who came on the boat didn't make it because they said it was too strict. You had to go to rehearsals on Tuesday and Friday mornings, and you got fined more for missing a rehearsal than you did for missing a night's work. You also had to play the music you had, and a lot of guys couldn't do it. I couldn't read so good in those days, but once I heard a number, that was all I needed. I stood by the piano at rehearsals so I could dig the chords from it.

The Streckfus people were funny to work for. You play music to suit them, not the public. As long as they were happy you had the job. You had 14 numbers to play in an evening, and you changed numbers every two weeks. The numbers were long. You'd play the whole number and maybe two or three encores and sometimes two choruses. A lot of guys didn't like that and quit. The Streckfus people made musicians out of a whole lot of guys that way. Louis Armstrong, Johnny St. Cyr, and I didn't know nothin' about reading' when we went on the boats, but we did when we came off. That's what started us off.

As long as I can remember, the Streckfuses had an excursion boat with a five-piece white band playing around New Orleans. It was called the *Belle of the Bend*. It went out every night and played a dance. They also had showboats that played the little towns around Louisiana.

Captain Johnny Streckfus came up with a name for us—the Jazz Syncopators. That's the first time I heard the name jazz. Later on in 1919 we changed the name to Fate Marable and His Jazz Maniacs. After that everybody started being jazz this and jazz that—Papa Celestin and His Jazz Band and like that. Before it was like Ory and His Ragtime Band. The Streckfus people always wanted us to play music at a tempo of 60 beats [per minute] or up. When you got down around 40 or 45, guys would be out on the floor doing nothing but shaking their butts very slow and dirty. The boats had floorwalkers looking for guys who were twisting themselves all up like that.

Arnold Metoyer played trumpet for a while on the boat when we were around New Orleans. He'd show up for the dance and say, "Man, my kid was sick so I had to hock my horn." Captain Johnny Streckfus would loan him the horn they kept on the boat and give him money to get his out. It kept happening all the time, so they finally made him leave his horn on the boat. Arnold loved to play kotch and would lose all his money trying to play it. When we were playing at Jim Tom's Road House in 1920, he'd always come out there saying he'd lost his horn. So we had to fire him.

Most of the times I worked on the boats in New Orleans, I also worked at longshore work during the week. The boats only worked on Friday night, two dances on Saturday, and at least one on Sunday. If there was a special party or something we'd play all day and then at night on Sunday. Sometimes you'd play special dates during the weeks. All the dances on the riverboats were for the whites except when we went to St. Louis, where we had ones for the colored on Monday nights. You'd pay 50 cents to get on and be given a little book for the 14 dances. You'd make notes in the book about who the dance was with and where you'd meet. Like by the left side of the pilothouse, or by the candy wheel, or downstairs at the bar. Most everybody came alone but left with somebody on their arm. It was a pleasure to see them having such a good time. Man, everybody was having fun in those days. The boat left at 9:00 P.M. and went downstream quite a ways, then started back to get in at 11:30 P.M. We started playing at 8:30 P.M. and played for an hour tied up at the dock. If I wasn't doing longshore work, we'd go to baseball games, the racetrack, or shoot pool during the day.

We got started playing on the boats just before the influenza epidemic of 1917. It hit and we had to lay off for a couple of months. We finished out that season, and then I did longshore work until 1918, when I went back on the boats. In 1918 we played the boats in New Orleans and got the band together to go to St. Louis in 1919.

Fate Marable was on the boats for the Streckfus people a long time before anybody else. He was practically raised on the boats because his mother worked on the boats when he was born. She was a maid on one of the boats they had to tow barges up and down the river. She would take care of the rooms for the crew. I never met Fate's mother, but I met his brother and sister. His brother worked at the soda fountain on the boats for a while, and he was around New York for a while. Fate was from Paducah, Kentucky, and in the summer he would go up the river on the steamer *Washington* on a tramp trip. They'd go all the way up the Mississippi to Dubuque, Iowa. They'd stay up the river for four months during summer, then come back to New Orleans for eight months. The river really froze up in winter. Fate played the piano and the steam calliope before any of the colored musicians went on the boats.

On May 3, 1919, I left New Orleans with Fate's band. We left on the train and got off at Paducah, Kentucky, to join the union because they didn't have any colored union in New Orleans. We stayed in the union one night and transferred to Local 44 in St. Louis. The next morning we caught the train to Rock Island, Illinois, to pick up the steamer St. Paul. We got to Rock Island May 5, 1919, and opened May 10, 1919, at Rock Island on the boat. While we were there they cut enough ice out of the river to last a month. They had a big saw, and guys would get out there and cut big blocks out for the freezer. Some of the guys like Peter Bocage didn't want to go to St. Louis, so they quit.

The boat carried no passengers or cargo; it was strictly for entertainment and for us to sleep on. Our pay was 35 dollars a week with room and board on the boat. In St. Louis it was 65 dollars a week and no room and board. When we first went on the boat with Fate it was $37.50 a week with no room and board. Our schedule was to Alton, Illinois, where we played a couple of nights, then there was a little town before Keokuk, Iowa, we played, then we played a couple of nights at Keokuk. We were the first big boat to go through the locks at Keokuk. We stopped at a little town called Louisiana, Missouri, and then went to Fort Madison, Des Moines, and Dubuque, Iowa. Later on we used to go up the Mississippi as far as St. Paul, Minnesota. We started back from Dubuque, and it sure was cold there. The boat had to hurry to be in St. Louis on May 30, which was Decoration Day. That was a big day. We stayed in St. Louis awhile before taking off again.

When we went on the boats in 1919, we had the greatest band from Dubuque, Iowa, to New Orleans. Even around St. Louis we were the best. They had some good musicians in St. Louis but no good bands. The Streckfus people had four bands on two boats running out of St. Louis, and none of them were from St. Louis. They had to send away to New Orleans, Chicago, Iowa, and Paducah, Kentucky, to get them. The two bands from Chicago were Louis Panico and Ralph Benson. The one from Paducah, Kentucky, was Percy Suggs, and from Iowa there was Tony and His Iowaians. Suggs and Tony played mostly on the steamer *Sydney*. Percy Suggs would get the boat in New Orleans and take it to Iowa, then Tony and his boys would take it on up the Ohio

River to Pittsburgh, Pennsylvania. All the bands were white except us and Suggs; we were the only colored. The white bands all had violins and played real sweet music. All the music I ever heard when we traveled was very tame. We hardly played any pop numbers after Louis Armstrong came on the boat. We started romping and played mostly ragtime like "Maple Leaf Rag," "Bag of Rags," "Champagne Rag." In St. Louis we could get all the ragtime music, and we played more of it than we did around New Orleans. They didn't seem to play rags anyplace else.

The Streckfus people had different boats and did quite a bit of shuffling of the bands on the boats. There was the *Capitol*, the *Sidney*, the *JS*, and the *St. Paul*. They tore up the *JS* after they got the *Capitol*. I played mostly on the steamer *St. Paul*. The *St. Paul* and the *Capitol* would play out of St. Louis and make trips up and down the Mississippi from St. Louis. One would go up the river and the other would go down. On the two boats playing around St. Louis, they had two bands. Benson's band and Tony and his Iowaians would leave on their boat about 8:00 P.M. and get back about 11:00 P.M. Our boat would leave about 11:30 P.M. The white guys came around to hear our music and they liked it. They'd all come over and get on our boat and have a good time.

Fate's band was called the night band on the steamer *St. Paul*. It was a tough band, and we had people lined up to get on the boat. When we first started playing in St. Louis, we had some guys always standing around the bandstand. We didn't know who they were but later on we found out they were guards. The Streckfus people thought we might have trouble from the white musicians and the gangsters, but we didn't have any. The Streckfus people wouldn't let us play any other jobs around St. Louis because they claimed the gangsters were after us. The gangsters weren't even thinking about us. The Streckfus people just didn't want us to get crowds anyplace but on the boats, and they thought we might quit and go someplace else. When we went to work for them, they had a little one-room shack down on the waterfront. After we went on the boats they moved downtown and took a whole floor of offices—we made them so much money. In the four months of summer in 1919, most of the time we worked from eight in the morning until 11:30 at night. That was long playing.

Besides the dances at night, they ran excursions during the day. For the dances at night one of the boats would go up the river and one down. The one going up the river would go as far as Alton, Illinois, and would take six hours to get there. Then they'd turn the boat around, start back; it took two hours to come down. The one going down the river would go as far as the army barracks—I think it was the Jefferson Barracks—and then come back. The *St. Paul* was known as the rough boat where they played jazz. The *Capitol* was known as a clean boat where they played sweet music. Each one had their own special crowd.

The Streckfus people liked to have a guy who fronted his own band. They had Fate, Charlie Creath, Dewey Jackson, Eddie Allen, and a guy named Floyd Campbell; he only lasted about a year. We all got paid by the Streckfus people, not by Fate or the other guys, and they did the hiring and firing. Fate got more than us because he was hired as leader. He would call the numbers and start them off, and conduct rehearsals. You had a book of numbers and you played them for a month. Then you got another set. We played the numbers different lengths; sometimes we'd play one chorus, sometimes three, and then we'd make different endings. Fate used to trick the band on new numbers. He'd get a new number and wouldn't show it to the band for a couple of days. He'd read it over and practice it on his lap every evening. Then on Friday rehearsal he'd show it to us, then sit down and play it like he could play it straight from the music.

I didn't learn how to read music good until I went to New York in 1929. Johnny St. Cyr and I used to have to really work on the numbers we played in Fate's band. On the boat they had a cashier who had a good ear for music. She used to keep a lead sheet, and when we hit a clinker she'd mark it down. Then the Streckfus people would make us do it right. We'd call the clinkers "blue notes." I got fired a whole lot of times off the boats and hired a lot of times. They didn't want Captain Johnny Streckfus to drink, and I'd sneak whiskey to him. I'd tie a string on a bottle and throw it over the back of the boat or hide it somewhere else. When Captain Johnny would get drunk he'd run around the boat and fire everybody but me. That made Captain Joe suspicious of me. One day in Dubuque, Iowa, he caught me and Captain Johnny with the whiskey hid under the seats. He was a hot baby, but he didn't fire me that time.

When we played little towns along the river, they'd advertise ahead of time what night we were stopping. We'd come in at about three in the afternoon, and Fate would be on top of the boat playing the steam calliope and everyone would be down at the river to see the boat come in. Then about 7:00 P.M. Fate would play the calliope again to let everyone know the boat's in town. There were two calliopes on the boat, the steam one on top and the electric one by the bandstand. Sometimes Fate would play the electric one with the band, but most times he'd play the piano. If you were standing next to those things you couldn't hear people talking for 15 or 20 minutes afterwards. Fate was a fair piano player who could read pretty good.

The riverboats had to lower their stacks when they went under a bridge. They'd lay the stacks right down on top of the boat. After they got under they'd raise them again. When you went to work on the boats you had to walk a little narrow plank to get aboard. If you wobbled or looked like you were drunk, they wouldn't let you come on the boat. Sometimes we'd be drunk and would fall off in the water.

At Fort Madison, Iowa, Johnny St. Cyr was going to have some teeth pulled, and I decided to have a couple pulled because Johnny was. The dentist said some of my back teeth needed pulling too. He pulled about seven of mine and a bunch of Johnny's. Neither one of us could eat for a week after that.

On July 4, 1919, Louis Armstrong, Johnny Dodds, and me got off the boat and went up a hill in St. Louis to Boots Saloon to get a half pint of whiskey each until Prohibition blew over. We didn't think it was going to last. On the boat they sold ice cream and soda pop, and they had a big freezer to keep it in. After Prohibition came, the bootleggers would keep their whiskey in the freezer and sell it on the boat.

The dances on the riverboats were segregated. Monday night out of St. Louis was for the colored. There were as many whites as colored on Monday nights, and you could hardly get on the boats that night. In New Orleans no colored were allowed on the boats. In Memphis and Pittsburgh sometimes they had colored on Monday nights. We called Mondays "getaway night" because you could get away with anything. The guys in the band would walk around smoking cigarettes and drinking and come down off the stand. On getaway night we used to nearly wreck the boat when we got to fighting. If a big fight breaks out in any dance hall, it's important you keep playing so the crowd won't panic. On the boats it's very important the people keep dancing. If they all run to one side of the boat, the boat'll tip over. It seems that most fights break out around the bandstand, and a lot of them want to get right up on the bandstand and fight. Usually you have three or four guys around the bandstand just to keep people from getting up on it. When the shootin' starts it gets rough. The first shootin' I was in was at McCall Plantation. Willie had just laid the bass down and started outside. One bullet went right through the string bass. I was outside and jumped in a barrel. The guy that did the shootin' ran past me and took off over a barbed-wire fence. He left about half his pants on the fence. On the boats the guys who acted up got put in the freezer with the ice cream and the soda pop. One guy started trouble when we were just getting goin'. He spent the whole evening there and was blue and stiff when he got out. Red McKenzie, the guy who blew the comb, used to be one of those little tough guys and was always standing at the bandstand getting in trouble. One night the bouncer hit him on top of the head, and he bounced right up into the bouncer's hand. I used to tell him later, "You got a very tough head."

Ernest Johnson was a bass player in one of the bands on the river. One day we were talking, and he said he had some chafing between his legs and wanted to know what to do about it. I told him to put some Sloane's

Liniment on it and rub it in, and that would cure it right. I never thought the guy would be crazy enough to do it. The poor guy did it and then jumped in the river to keep from burning up. He couldn't walk for a week. He was gonna shoot me over it.

There were four colored bass players on the boats. I was the first, then Jim Johnson, Henry Kimball who I admired so much, and then Al Morgan, Sam's brother, who got a job way late. Isaac Jefferson was a piano player who worked the boats with us and was very good. Burroughs Lovingood was another guy that played piano very good. The last time I saw Isaac he had a good job in Detroit in the '30s. With Fate we had a very good trombone player named U.S. Grant Cooper. He was about the size of Jimmy Archey and looked like him. We needed a guy who could read music good and he could. Before him we had Bebe Ridgley for about a month. But he quit and went back to New Orleans. Grant Cooper wasn't any fly trombone player, but he could play what he saw. Later on he was with Charlie Creath. We got Louis Armstrong out of the Ory Band to work with us. Louis was the only one out of Ory's band who could read at all, and Louis couldn't read so good. Joe Howard, one of the old trumpet players in Fate's band, gave Louis a lot of help. Louis should give Joe a whole lot of credit. Dave Jones, the mellophone player in the band, helped Louis too. Dave played as much music on mellophone as Louis did on trumpet. He wanted to play sax though, just like I wanted to play tuba, and no one could tell me anything. Another guy who helped Louis was Sam Dutrey. Later on Lil Armstrong helped Louis a lot. Lil played a whole lot of piano. Louis can read very good now.

Some of those old records just don't move me at all. Like the one my brother's on with Fate—it stinks. If you try to play like those guys did back then, you're dead. After we got back to New Orleans in 1919, the Streckfus people hired another bunch of guys for Fate's band. I think the only guys that were left were Louis Armstrong and Baby Dodds. Baby left soon after that.

The opening paragraphs of the next chapter furnish the jazz historian with valuable information. The enlargement of the small jazz band into the 10- or 12-piece dance orchestra was part of the inevitable commercialization of New Orleans music. Pops places the date as early as 1921. Brass and reed sections were doubled or even tripled, and saxophones were introduced to smooth out the overall sound of the band. The old New Orleans front line with its functional cornet-trombone-clarinet instrumentation would eventually disappear; the saxophone would overpower and eventually doom the clarinet. The greater instrumentation created difficulties for contrabassists; as Pop relates, he bought and began playing his first tuba in 1921. Only the brass bass possessed sufficient power to drive the rhythm sections of the new dance orchestras, or so the leaders and music contractors thought. It would be several years before Pops stopped doubling and convinced bandleaders that the string bass was indeed the most suitable instrument for the rhythm section.

No trace of the glass recordings made by the Gold Whispering Band has ever been found, but Pops's disclosure will undoubtedly set collectors on the shadowy trail. Pops's tenure with the inflated Eddie Allen Orchestra, apparently not much to his liking, marked the end of his first riverboat period. Several New Orleans jazzmen who had gone to the West Coast reported good jobs to be had in that part of the country, and Pops accepted trombonist Kid Ory's invitation to join a band working at the One Eleven in Los Angeles. The place of employment proved to be a taxi-dance hall. (Pops's recollection notwithstanding, the location was most likely 111 West Third Street, since Main and Spring are parallel.) The area was then known for its dime-a-dance parlors, rather sedate versions of the New Orleans cabaret. Customers paid ten cents for the privilege of dancing with glamorous hostesses; the dances lasted about 60 seconds each, requiring constant changes of tunes and tempo. After the job with Kid Ory at the One Eleven, Pops worked with Papa Mutt Carey, a fine New Orleans trumpeter, at the Liberty on Third Street east of Main. Los Angeles proved to a be dull place. Although Ory and Carey stayed on, Pops returned in 1923 to St. Louis, which had become a familiar secondary base of operations during his riverboat period. Musical activity was on a level only below that in Chicago and New York. Charlie Creath and Dewey Jackson were booking Negro orchestras; Frankie Trumbauer had a dazzling band at the Arcadia Ballroom with Bix Beiderbecke, Pee Wee Russell and, briefly, Jack Teagarden and Peck Kelley. The only untoward aspect of working in St. Louis was that jazz bands were really dance orchestras, cut in the new style and tailored to the requirements of ballroom audiences. The pure New Orleans style was being submerged. Pops began playing tuba again.

In 1924 Pops made his first phonograph records for Okeh, as a member of the Charlie Creath Jazz-O-Maniacs. A man named Ralph Peer headed the artists-and-repertoire department of Okeh and was in charge of building a jazz and blues catalog to exploit the "race" market. Okeh had established studio facilities in a building in downtown St. Louis, augmenting its main studios in Chicago. The label and Peer were responsible for much of the best jazz recorded in the early years; in addition to recording Charlie Creath and Dewey Jackson, Okeh achieved an important first with the Bennie Moten Orchestra from Kansas City, all of these sessions being conducted in St. Louis. Among the important artists to visit Okeh's Chicago facilities were New Orleans jazzmen King Oliver, Louis Armstrong, Johnny Dodds, Freddie Keppard, Clarence Williams, and Sidney Bechet. In later years original Okeh 78-rpm recordings became prime objects of searches by jazz collectors. The label stayed in business until forced into bankruptcy during the Depression.

Pops Foster made a total of 15 titles in St. Louis. In December 1924 and March 1925 he was a member of Creath's eight-piece band. In November 1925 the Creath Jazz-O-Maniacs had been increased to ten pieces with the welcome addition of Lonnie Johnson on violin and Zutty Singleton on drums. In 1926 Pops was anchorman in the rhythm section of the Dewey Jackson Peacock Orchestra, which cut three titles for Vocation in June 1926 and an additional two titles for Okeh, in May 1927. The May engagement benefited from the addition of trombonist Albert Wynn, reedman Horace Eubanks, and Burroughs Lovingood, a veteran pianist and calliope player from the riverboats. Pops played tuba on all 15 sides. The music recorded was of good quality but lacked the brilliant solo work heard on performances by King Oliver and other more definitive authentic New Orleans bands playing in Chicago.

Reading between the lines, one gathers that life in St. Louis was pleasant for Pops, although the musical associations left something to be desired. One day at the Okeh recording studios Clarence Williams told Pops, "You ain't got no business here," suggesting that he seek faster company and perhaps try New York. Pops did not go East yet, but his travels began once more. After a six-month stint on the riverboats, Pops returned to New Orleans for a job with Sidney Desvignes. A footloose period followed; there were jobs with Creath in St. Louis; Mutt Carey, Lips Page, and the Elks Brass Band in Los Angeles; Desvignes again in New Orleans and on the boats; and finally with Dewey Jackson in St. Louis. Such frequent changes of bands and locales were very much a part of the life of the jazzman in those days. Not until 1929 did Pops finally take Clarence Williams's advice and push on to New York for the longest and most important affiliation of his career, with the Luis Russell Orchestra.

—Ross Russell

Chapter 8
Prohibition

"On Saturdays we'd drive someplace like down to Watts and buy some bootleg whiskey from the cops."

❧

In 1920 I fooled around with Ory's band, Bab Frank's band at Jim Tom's Road House, and the Tuxedo Band. Then in 1921, before the season opened, Charlie Creath sent for me and Johnny St. Cyr to go to work on the steamer *St. Paul*. We gave the Tuxedo Band a two-month, two-week notice. Then when we left Bebe Ridgley said, "Hate to see you go, man, you coulda stayed with us; you guys are dirty." Everybody liked Papa Celestin, but the guys didn't like Ridgley and he had the band. They finally split off. Ridgley had the Original Tuxedo Band, and Papa Celestin had Celestin's Original Tuxedo Band. Papa Celestin hired Emma Barrett as his piano player, and she was the only woman I knew who played in a band. Then the bass player left Ridgley and started the Young Tuxedo Band. For a while there were a gang of Tuxedo bands around New Orleans.

I worked a month with Charlie, and the Streckfus people put me with Eddie Allen's band. That was the year I first started playing tuba. I bought my own in 1921. They built the band around Eddie Allen and called it the Gold Whispering Band. That was the first time they started using soprano, tenor, and alto saxophones. Before that they were all C-melody horns. We had Harry Lankford, trombone; Sidney Desvignes, trumpet; Floyd Casey, drums; Eddie Allen, trumpet; Johnny

St. Cyr, banjo; Isaac Jefferson, piano; Walter Thomas; alto, Norman Mason, alto; me on tuba; and Gene Sedric, tenor. We called the band Eddie Allen's Gold Whispering Band. Part of that year I worked in Eddie Allen's band on days and Fate's band at night.

When I got back to New Orleans with the Gold Whispering Band, we cut some cylinders at somebody's house off Perdido Street. It was one of those old windup things. They were glass records. Two of the tunes we made were "Hot Lips" and "When Hearts Were Young." We made a bunch of tunes that day. I never heard them. Darnell Howard did, and he said they came out good. Johnny St. Cyr had the cylinders.

I played with the Gold Whispering Band around New Orleans for a while, and I jobbed around with other bands. It was around that time that Johnny Dunn came down to New Orleans and got stranded there. I played with him a few times while he was there. Dunn came from Memphis, and I didn't think much of his style—just a wa-wa-wa style. There were some blues singers from Memphis too. But the good ones came out of those little backwood places like the plantations and cottonfields of Mississippi and from the railroads. Guys working on the railroad sang some good blues. Around New Orleans women sang the blues and no men sang them.

Kid Ory had taken part of his band to Los Angeles by then. Mutt Carey, Eddie Garland, and Ory had gone. They hired Dink Johnson, who was already out there, and a couple of other guys. Montudie and Ory got in a fight like they always did. Montudie went to work for the Black and Tan Band, and Ory didn't have a bass player. He wrote to me to come out. I wanted to get away from my first wife, Bertha, so I went. Back then if a bandleader wanted you to play with him, he'd write and send you money for the trip. After you started working you had to pay it back.

When I got out to California, Montudie saw me and said, "What are you doin' out here George? This ain't no place for you." He didn't want me out here and wanted me to go back to New Orleans. He and Ory fought so much I think Ory's band was without a bass player most of the time. Those two guys would fight about anything. Stuff was always flying around, like, "Man, why don't you cut it out and learn how to play." "Hey, Montudie, where'd you get that silly hat?" "Why don't you learn how to blow that horn." "You're jealous of me, man, you're too cheap to even buy a hat." "Straighten up your cap, man." Stuff like that would go on all the time. The last fight they had when I was with them was at the Club Hangover in San Francisco. We were up on a raised bandstand. They got to arguing, and Montudie pushed Ory off the back of the bandstand where they stored the empty bottles. Ory nearly got killed. He cracked some ribs and got cut up. They've always been the best of friends.

While I was with Ory we played the One Eleven Dance Hall near Main and Spring. We played at night from 8:00 P.M. to 11:30 P.M. during the week. Saturday night it was from 8:00 P.M. to 1:00 A.M. On Sundays L.A. really closed up. The only things on the street were police, ambulance, and fire trucks. If you wanted to go out of town you had to get a permit. On Sunday nights the dance hall didn't open until midnight. In the band we had Ory; Papa Mutt, trumpet; Fred Washington, piano; Bud Scott, banjo; Bonner, saxophone; Billy Butler, saxophone, and me on string bass and tuba.

We always called Ory "Dut." Nobody I remember from those days called him Ory or Kid. Bonner the saxophone player and me decided to buy a car and put up 75 dollars apiece. I couldn't drive, but I was supposed to have the car on Saturday and him on Sunday. He had a family and wanted to take them riding on Sunday. I never did learn how to drive, so he used to drive me. On Saturdays we'd drive someplace like down to Watts and buy some bootleg whiskey from the cops. In those days Watts was known as Leake's Lake.

Frankie Dusen and his band came out to L.A. in 1922. They had Buddy Petit on trumpet, L.Z. Cooper on piano, and a little guy named Pills

Coycault on clarinet. Pills was Ernest "Nenny" Coycault's brother. Nenny had come out to California way early and had started playing with the Black and Tan Band. They were the only band who played ragtime for a long time out here. Frankie's band was playing in a theater. The first week they played their music and the people raved over them. The next week the vaudeville acts came in and they had to play music for the acts. None of them could read and that was it. Frank told me later he went back to the place where he was living with some people. They were cooking some beans with a big ham hock in it. He said he went in and it sure smelled good. He couldn't wait for the beans so he stole the ham hock, wrapped it up in a paper, went on, and caught the train back to New Orleans with the ham hock.

I got tired of playing with a band that couldn't read, so I left Ory in the fall of 1923 and went back to St. Louis to play with Charlie Creath. Charlie had several bands going. He had all of Missouri and southern Illinois sewed up. We even went up to Chicago and played a few gigs. One of his bands was still playing the boats. The boats were so crowded on Saturdays the crew and the band would go on the back of the boat so the insurance man wouldn't count us in the limit of 500 people. Sometimes they'd get 700 or 800 people on the boat. It would be so loaded the least little wave would wash over on the deck. One time in Davenport, Iowa, one guy bet another guy ten dollars he wouldn't jump overboard. He did, and everybody ran to that side of the boat. The band was on a break and we started playing right away to get the people dancing. One of the guards pulled out his pistol and shot it a couple of times to scare the people into moving. They put the guy that jumped in jail.

Every band Charlie sent out wanted a bass player, and I was the only bass player around St. Louis. He'd get extra money when he sent me, but he didn't tell me. I found out about it one night when I didn't want to go on a job. He kept beggin' me so hard I knew somethin' was up, so when I played the place I asked the guy what he paid Charlie, and he told me he had to pay quite a bit more for the bass. I went to

Charlie and told him I wasn't goin' out no more unless he paid me extra. He did.

The only other band around St. Louis was Willie Austin until Dewey Jackson took off on his own. There were a few little bands that just had violin, guitar, and one or two other instruments. Charlie had the area all sewed up. At one time he had about ten bands all pulling the dough in for him. He was so busy he only made appearances at the biggest jobs. He had a big Marmon car he drove around from job to job. He'd stop at the job, play a number with the band and leave. A lot of people thought Dewey Jackson was Charlie because he played a lot more jobs than Charlie did. Bob Schoffner did a lot of playing for him too. Charlie could play very good. He's the only trumpet player I ever saw that never pulled out the tuning shank on the trumpet. He never even tested it. If he wanted a sharp or a flat he just licked it on the mouthpiece and blew. He had a strong lip and a nice reputation. He played straight and powerful. He ruined himself, though.

The first time I met Coleman Hawkins was in St. Louis about 1923. He was with Fletcher Henderson's band at the Coliseum. We liked to run them out of gas with Dewey on trumpet. Dewey is very fast at fingering and plays long, straight, powerful notes like Charlie. Dewey played with a mute most of the time. Whenever a rough new trumpet player would come to St. Louis on a traveling show and wanted to cut the guys, we'd send for Dewey. He was a rough baby. The guys from Fletch's band came around to see us; I was slapping the bass real hard and looked up. Hawk and a lot of other guys were watching me. After I got down they started saying, "Man, that's great, you should come to New York and play with us." I told them I was doing all right in St. Louis.

I met Bix when he was playing the Arcadia Ballroom with Trumbauer, Rod Cless, Pee Wee Russell, and those guys about 1923. Bix and Pee Wee lived over in Granite City, Illinois. On Mondays all the musicians had the day off and used to all go over there to see who could burn up the most barbecue. They didn't have a regular barbecue; we just dug a hole in the ground, put rocks in then some wood, and got a fire going. We'd cook the barbecue, eat it, and drink a lot of corn whiskey. We never played or jammed together in those days; that all started in New York. We just got together for kicks. The colored and white musicians were just one. We'd stay out all night, drink out of the same bottle, and go out with the same girls. We used to all pile in Bix's car and go over to Kattie Red's in East St. Louis and drink a lot of bad whiskey. It was green whiskey, man. They sure had bad stuff, but none of us ever got sick on it. I heard Bix play trumpet and piano and he was good. Trumbauer was a nice guy and a wonderful saxophone player. Him and Trumbauer never came around to sit in with us even in New York. One of the few white guys who used to sit in with us in New York was Jack Teagarden.

Around 1923 the delegate of Local 44 got a one-night job over at Beardstown, Illinois, for a little pickup band. It was a little coal-mining town where the miners come in and bring a jug to drink on all night. This one big tough guy with a long mustache came carrying a crock jug over his shoulder. He was unshaven, dirty, and chewed tobacco, and sat in a chair he'd pulled right in front of the bandstand. He laid a big pistol in his lap and told us to play nothin' but "Yes We Got No Bananas." We started playing it, and the guy who put on the dance came up and told us to do what the guy wanted or he'd break the dance up. All night long we played "Yes We Got No Bananas" and the people there danced to it. Sometimes during the evening he'd want us to drink with him and would pass the jug up. None of us wanted to drink behind him, but we did. He'd sit there and sing to the music, twirl the pistol on his finger, and point it at us. Once in a while he'd get up to go to the bathroom. He'd stand up and tell us to stop playing and not to hit a lick until he got back. We didn't care how long he stayed, we waited until he got back. When he came back he'd say, "All right, fellas, let's go," and we'd start playing. After all the people left he asked us if we had a good time. We all said yes. I never will forget that guy, and 50 years later I still can't play "Yes We Got No Bananas" without nearly getting sick.

Some of the other trumpet players around St. Louis were Big Bob, a guy named Crackter, and Benny Washington. Wellman Braud carried Crackter to New York after Braud left Duke. They were all good. Bob Schoffner was one of the best trumpet players besides Charlie and Dewey. I remember when he was playing around with us in Charlie's band. He came up to Johnny St. Cyr and me and said he knew we were from New Orleans and wondered if he could get some charm for luck to gamble with. A lot of the guys in those days thought anybody from New Orleans knew voodoo, magic, and all that junk. Johnny told him, "Yeah, man, George here can fix you up." I told him, "Yeah, man, I'll fix you up." I got my landlady to cut up a nice square piece of red flannel from some old underwear and sew it in a pouch. Inside I put a lump of coal and rosin. I told Bob I had to have $9.15 for it, and the money had to be nine silver dollars and three nickels, and I wouldn't take it any other way. When he got the charm I told him not to look at it for nine days or it would break the spell. He went right out and started gambling and lost all of his money. He looked at the charm and the next night he came up on the bandstand with a shotgun wrapped in a tablecloth, wanting his money back. He was really hot. I gave him the money back and told him he must've crabbed his luck by looking at the charm. He said he had looked, and then he wanted me to make him another one. I told him, "No, man, I don't think your hand is right. Let me look at it." I looked at it and told him, "No, man, it's impossible. You already broke your luck charm."

When we used to make records in St. Louis, they'd hire a loft in one of the downtown store buildings. The band would practice without the bass and drums. We'd sit over to one side having some fun until they were ready for us. Then we'd play with the rest of the band and cut the records. They had big megaphones going into the wall. We'd stand up to the megaphone and play. The wax was cut on the other side of the wall. If you cut a hog you had to start all over and cut the wax again. Clarence Williams got to be in charge of the colored music for the Okeh Company, and he used to go all over the country hunting for blues singers. He's the one that carried Lonnie Johnson to New York. Clarence came down to St. Louis one time we were cutting records with Charlie Creath's band. When he saw me he said, "You ain't got no business here; you should come to New York where you can do better." I said I might do that someday. The other guys said, "We're doing all right here with Foster."

Those days with Charlie Creath were really good ones. I lived at Charlie's house with him, his wife Pauline, and his sister Marge. When Charlie would get paid off from jobs he'd pay me and the other guys off, then he'd go lose his money gambling. Then he'd send Pauline around to ask me for a loan for the rent money. I'd say, "Charlie's mad at me and not even talking to me. I can't be loaning money to no one that's not talking to me." He'd pop up and say, "What do you mean not talking to you? You'd better pay the rent." I'd go on outside in the street for a while and then I'd give Pauline the money and tell her not to let Charlie know. When we were up on the road playing a date, the band would usually get together and gamble. I'd get lucky sometimes and win all the money. Charlie would get mad. I'd tell him that I was gonna take Marge and ride the train home and he could go in the car. They'd be so broke they didn't even have gas money. He'd come around before Marge and I left, saying, "Hey, George, we haven't got any gas for the car." I'd say, "Man, I don't need any gas. Marge and I are taking the train back." He'd start being sweet and saying, "Aww, don't be like that." I'd loan him five until we got back.

Charlie was a good guy; he just did himself a whole lot of harm. He loved to gamble more than anything. Mostly he played stud poker and dice. He never knew when to quit. He'd only quit when he was broke. Then he'd get all clean and brush himself off. Chasing women was another one of Charlie's problems. He left a good wife for a tramp. Then he got caught white-slaving girls from St. Louis to Chicago. Charlie just kept going down. He got so bad he was living around there with a queer so he could eat and had a job sweeping the decks of the riverboats. In 1938 when I was with Louis Armstrong in Chicago, I got a note from him saying he was in the Bridewell—that's the jailhouse in Chicago—and for me to send him all the money I could because he needed plenty of it. I wrote him back telling him I could use all the money I could get too.

⚜

About 1925 I got a job with Dewey Jackson's band on the boats. We played around St. Louis and went up the river. Dewey is about as old a guy as I am, and I'd been staying with him since 1919. Dewey was very fast at fingering and had good syncopation, but didn't have much tone. His band was a good romping band. I played with Dewey's band for about six months, and then the Streckfus people fired me. Charlie Creath wouldn't hire me after that because I'd gone with Dewey. My brother told me to come home and I could work in Sidney Desvignes's band, so I did.

I worked with Sidney's band until 1927. On Tuesday and Friday we played a club, Wednesday and Thursday we played Uptown, and Sunday we played at the lake. We also traveled around the country a lot playing in Mississippi and Alabama. We played a lot of school dates over there. New Orleans bands had been traveling since way early. I remember around 1914 or 1915 I played Dallas, Texas, with the Original Tuxedo Band. The New Orleans Pelicans were in the Southern Baseball League, and we went over to play for the team. Both teams were white. It was around 1926 that Sidney's band got an offer to go to Miami, Florida, to play a job. That was just after Jack Carter's band had been down there and one of his guys got killed from being tarred and feathered. Jack's band was from around Chicago, and he'd played drums in Noble Sissle's band. Some of the guys in Jack's band tried to teach some white girls to dance at the place they were playing. This gang of white guys didn't like it, so they played like they wanted to hire them for an extra date later that night. When they got there, they really got it. Somebody in Sidney's band knew the chief of police in Miami, and they called down there to see if he would give us protection. He said he couldn't because down there they didn't want colored playing for white, and we didn't go.

Later on when I went back to Los Angeles I found out Jack Carter had taken a band to Shanghai, China. He took Darnell Howard and Albert Nicholas with him. A lot of guys would get jobs on boats from the West Coast, and when they got to China they'd jump the boat and get a job playing.

We had Sidney Desvignes and Gene Ware on trumpet, Eddie Cherie on tenor and clarinet, Ory Umphrey on trombone, Tuton on alto, Louis Barbarin on drums, me on bass, and my brother on banjo and violin. In early 1927 Willie left for New York to join Joe Oliver, and we got John Marrero on banjo and violin. Sidney was a straight trumpet player and could read very good. His tone was green and was hardly no tone at all. He wasn't a very good trumpet player.

The whole band went to Mobile, Alabama, to play a job about 1927. When we got there they sent me over to a very nice room, but Louis Barbarin heard about it and took off to get there before I did. Louis rented it out from under me, and when I got there he was out in front telling the guys how good the room was and how soft the bed was. I skipped around back and loaded his bed up with firewood and coal. He brought the guys in to see it and ran over and jumped on the bed. After he hit it he sure was hot. He said he was gonna kill the guy who did it if he found him.

On the way back to New Orleans that time we met Sam Morgan's band. They had hit a detour in the road they were on and had gotten lost. Isaiah Morgan, who couldn't talk so plain, hollered at us that they would be a lot further if there hadn't been a "Detroit" in the road. We got him to say it several times and then we all cracked up laughing; we thought it was very funny.

❦

A lot of the time I was with Sidney we worked on the *Island Queen*. It was owned by a Captain Scholtz out of Philadelphia. In the summer of 1926 we went up the river on the boat. We got up there and fooled around so long the river got low and we couldn't get out. If the river was too high you couldn't get under the bridges, and if it got too low you hit bottom. We came back down to New Orleans on the train until the boat could get out, when we went back and got it and came down the river. In 1927 Sidney's band was playing at the Peaceman's Temple, and Papa Mutt came to New Orleans to visit and asked me to go back to L.A. and play with him. I went.

Papa Mutt had taken over Ory's band and changed the name to the Liberty Syncopators. We played the Liberty Dance Hall on Third Street between Los Angeles and Main streets. We had Minor Hall on drums—we called him "Ram"—Joe Darensbourg played clarinet, and Leon White—who played drums way early with the Black and Tan Band—on trombone. I was on bass and Papa Mutt was on trumpet.

Ram was a funny guy that I had some fun with one time. He came around telling us he was getting a hard-on every night on the bandstand. I told him to tie a string around it just before he went on the stand. He really tied it around and then went on. Pretty soon the whole thing started tightening on him and in a few minutes he ran screaming off the stand. He couldn't get the string untied, and he had one helluva time getting it loose. When he got back all the guys really kidded him.

While I was playing with Papa Mutt I got to the dance hall early one night. I decided I would go down and play the Chinese lottery. The Chinamen had a restaurant with a back room and a counter where you went to play the lottery. As I was going in a couple of guys were coming out. They said, "Going to try your luck, man?" And I said, "Yeah." When I got to the back room there wasn't anybody there. I stood around and called for a minute before I heard somebody knocking in a closet. I opened the closet, and out fell Ram and two great big Chinamen all tied together. I started laughing, and Ram started yelling at me to untie him or he was going to punch me in the mouth. I laughed some more and finally untied them. The place had been robbed by the guys I'd met on the way in.

Papa Mutt and Jimmy Archey were the two funniest guys I knew. When they lived with Alma and me in New York, Alma lost about 25 pounds laughing at their jokes. She'd be laughing so hard she'd forget to eat. Mutt loved to tell about a drummer and an alto player he had. They both stammered. When they met for the first time the drummer said, wh-wh-ah-ah-when e-e-ever ya-ya-you're ready ta-ta-ta-to s-s-s-start." The alto player said, "Ya-ya-ya-you m-m-m-m-mockin' m-m-m-me," and they started fighting.

The Black and Tan Band in Los Angeles was the only band around there playing ragtime for a long time. I never worked with them, but I knew them all. Ernest Nenny Coycault played trumpet with them and came from Breakaway, Louisiana. He played around New Orleans and then came out here way early. Later on he was with Sonny Clay's band. Way late he changed his name to Ernest Johnson. Their drummer was Leon White, who played trombone with us in Papa Mutt's band. He was a nice trombone player, very good. Jim Jackson was their piano player, but later he switched to tuba because he couldn't play enough piano. Paul Howard and Leon Herriford played saxes and clarinet. I worked some jobs with them, and they were with Reb Spikes for a while. Harry Southard was the leader and played trombone. He was a good trombone player and owned a barbershop in L.A. He was also the Conn instrument dealer around there.

I think the Black and Tan Band made some records around L.A. before Ory did, and I think Curtis Mosby played drums on the records. Curtis had a band around L.A. for a long time. I played some of the big parties with them when I was there in 1922. Fatty Arbuckle used to give a bunch of wild parties we played. Curtis was more of a promoter than a musician and wasn't too good on drums. When the band had to play the big shows, Curtis hired Lionel Hampton to play drums. Leon Herriford played first alto and Les Hite played second alto. Paul Howard played first tenor. All the saxes doubled on clarinet. They had Parker Berry, who was an outstanding trombone player from Cincinnati. There was another trombone player named Tin Can Henry Allen. Willie Porter and a guy named Meyers were on trumpets. Meyers was a light guy from Kansas City. Henry Starr was the piano player and did the vocals in the band.

Henry Starr was a very good-looking guy with straight blond hair and grey eyes. You didn't know whether he was white or colored. He had several girls on the line for him and considered himself a pimp and hustler. Music was just a sideline for him, and the band couldn't keep up with him. Henry would be with some chick and wouldn't show up or say he didn't feel good and couldn't make it. He was a cute guy and they could never find him, so they sent to New Orleans for Walter Jacobs to come out and play with them. One night Starr walked in the theater and found Jacobs playing the piano. He straightened out after that and stayed with Mosby. Both Starr and Jacobs could play the piano and sing, so they traded off. I used to do a lot of party jobs around town with Walter and Henry. There would be piano and bass music, and one of the guys would sing. Henry was originally from San Francisco and was a very good piano player.

Curtis had a very nice band. They played the Lincoln Theater and other places for the little TOBA shows. In 1927 Les Hite formed a band to go into Frank Sebastian's Cotton Club and wanted me to go with them. I told them I wouldn't go unless they took our whole band, so we didn't get the job. I think Les Hite had a better band than Crosby's. Curtis ended up in San Francisco, and in the 1950s he had a little club on Eddy Street where I used to go see him sometimes. He died in the '50s.

When I was in California I was supposed to go to Australia with Sonny Clay's band for ten months. I didn't go and they ended up staying only ten days. Australia is the worst Jim Crow country in the world, and the musicians over there didn't want them to play. Over there colored weren't supposed to have any white girls in their rooms. The white musicians hired some white girls to get friendly with Sonny Clay's boys and get in their rooms. When the party got going good one of the girls pulled a window shade down, and that was the sign for the cops to come in. They knocked on the door "to let them in in the name of the King." The cops took them all to the stockade and then shipped each guy out on a separate boat. Some went to Bogalusa, some went to Texas, and about everywhere but where they started from. That was around 1922, and after that Sonny came back to California and started another band. He was playing there in 1927.

Lips Page came out to California way early and made some records. They had an old bus that had wheels like a covered wagon. I made the records with him. They used the name Papa Midnight and His Band. Lips couldn't use his name because he worked for another record company.

In September 1928 I left Los Angeles with the Elks Brass Band playing tuba. We had Teddy Hill on piano and tenor sax. We needed him to play piano at night at dances, so we got him a job playing the sax in the band during the day. He marched in the band and held the horn up like he was playing it. We played San Francisco, Oakland, Salt Lake City, Kansas City, St. Louis, and went on to Chicago. In Chicago I stayed with Johnny St. Cyr and all his babies. He wanted me to stay and play around Chicago. I looked into it but would've had to wait until all the other bass players in town got a job before I'd get one. I went on back to St. Louis and joined Dewey Jackson all over again.

I stayed with Dewey Jackson until 1929. I lived with Jesse Johnson while I was there. Louis Metcalf had seen me in St. Louis and told Luis Russell about me. Luis Russell sent me a telegram wanting me to join him in New York. Jesse Johnson got the telegram and kept it for three weeks before he gave it to me. Jesse did all the booking for bands and entertainments around St. Louis and was a good friend of Dewey's and didn't want to see me go. Jesse and his wife, Edith, had a fight, and she told me to make Jesse give me my telegram. I used to fool around with Edith before Jesse married her, and he was always accusing me of fooling with her. He used to carry a pistol and say he was gonna shoot me for fooling with her. I'd tell him, "When you catch me right you can shoot."

After I got the telegram and found out Luis Russell wanted me, I sent myself a telegram saying "Come home at once," and left for New York on February 11, 1929. After I got to New York I used to send extra sheet music to Dewey and the guys around St. Louis. Dewey wrote me some years ago saying he'd got religious and joined the Sanctified Church. He said he was only playing for the Lord.

Louis Armstrong in the 1930s. The top photo is signed
"To Fireman George Foster."

148

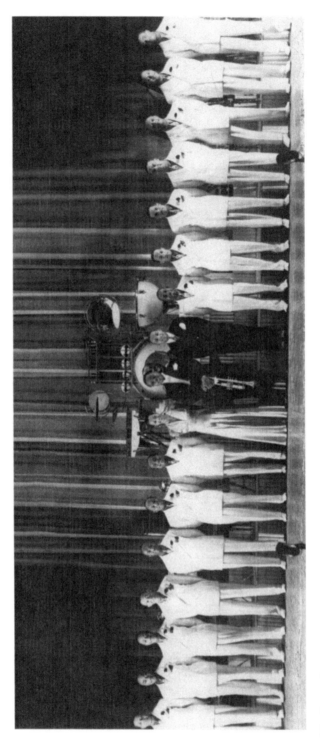

The Louis Armstrong Orchestra, about 1936. From left: Henry "Red" Allen, trumpet; Lee Blair, guitar; Louis Bacon, trumpet; Pops Foster, bass; unknown; Luis Russell, piano, Gus Aiken, trumpet; Bobby Caston, vocals; Louis Armstrong, trumpet; Sonny Woods, vocals; Jimmy Archey, trombone; Charles Holmes, reeds; Greely Walton, reeds; Paul Barbarin, drums; Bingie Madison, reeds; Henry "Moon" Jones, reeds; Leonard "Ham" Davis, trumpet.

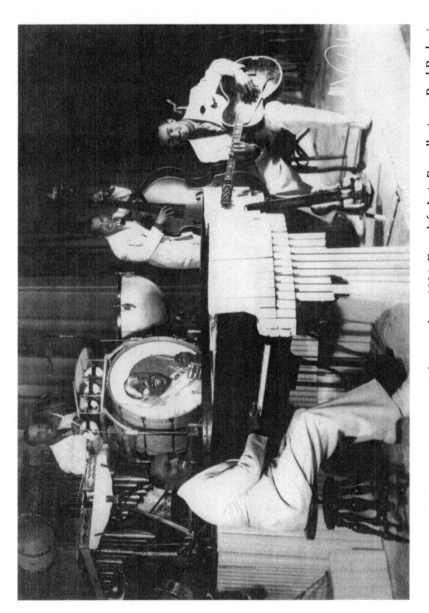

Rhythm section of the Louis Armstrong Orchestra, about 1936. From left: Luis Russell, piano; Paul Barbarin, drums; Pops Foster, bass; Lee Blair, guitar.

150

Midge Williams, late 1930s.

Pops Foster, about 1936, after recovering from a long illness.

Sonny Woods, about 1935.

Barney Bigard, late 1940s.

Alpha and Louis Armstrong and Alma and Pops Foster on an outing at Coney Island, New York, about 1934.

Part of the Louis Armstrong Orchestra, about 1936. From left: Paul Barbarin, drums; Louis Armstrong, trumpet; Henry Jones, reeds; Lee Blair, guitar; Pops Foster, string bass.

Willie Bunk Johnson, San Francisco, about 1945, shortly after his rediscovery and rehabilitation.

154

Jimmy Archey and His Jazz Band, New York, about 1945. Henry Goodwin, trumpet; Tommy Benford, drums; Jimmy Archey, trombone; Dick Wellstood, piano; Benny Waters, clarinet; Pops Foster, bass.

Pops and Willie Foster, about 1950.   *Pops and Alma, Boston, 1945.*

The Foster family, about 1945. From left: Alma, Annie, Elizabeth, and Pops.

New Orleans musicians' get-together, 1944. From left: Big Eye Louis Nelson, clarinet; Walter Decou, trombone; Peter Bocage, cornet; Paul Barbarin, drums; Louis Keppard, banjo; Pops Foster, bass; Sidney Bechet, clarinet and soprano saxophone; Alphonse Picou, clarinet.

The Sidney Bechet Band in Boston, 1945. From left: George Thompson, drums; Pops Foster, bass; Bunk Johnson, trumpet; Sidney Bechet, soprano saxophone; Ray Parker, piano.

Pops in 1945.

Jimmy Archey
and Pops Foster
in Sweden, 1956.

Pops at Club Hangover,
Bush and Powell streets,
San Francisco, about
1956. The band was led
by pianist Earl "Fatha"
Hines and featured cor-
netist Muggsy Spanier.
Joe Sullivan was the
intermission pianist.

Pops in Zurich,
Switzerland, 1956.

New Orleans Jazz Group on tour in Europe, about 1965.
From left: Alton Parnell, Jimmy Archey (with glasses):,
Darnell Howard, Alvin Alcorn, Josiah Frazier, Pops Foster.

Eddie "Montudie" Garland and Wellman Braud, 1966.

160

Warren "Baby" Dodds, about 1950.

Minor Hall, about 1945.

Pops and Alma, 1960.

The Luis Russell Orchestra was a quality jazz band. That it did not attain the eminence of Fletcher Henderson or Duke Ellington was perhaps as much a matter of luck as anything else. The band swung well and did not lack for solo talent: Henry Red Allen, Louis Metcalf, Rex Stewart, trumpets; J.C. Higginbotham, trombone; Albert Nicholas, Teddy Hill, Omer Simeon, Barney Bigard, and Charlie Holmes, reeds. Luis Russell was a Panamanian with an interesting history. The son of a church choir director and piano teacher, he had won $3,000 in a lottery when he was 17, using the money to migrate in 1919 with part of his family to New Orleans where he fit quickly into the musical scene. Russell joined the exodus of New Orleans musicians to Chicago in the early '20s and, after various affiliations with name bands there and in St. Louis, arrived in New York, where he launched a band of his own.

Russell did not ask Pops to play tuba; he was too sound a New Orleans musician for that. Pops abandoned the brass bass instruments for good and concentrated on the string bass. By this time he had developed three main techniques on the instrument: the conventional arco and pizzicato methods, plus a unique slapped technique, whereby the fretboard was struck simultaneously with the strings, creating a strong tone with great carrying power. It was just the effect needed to install the contrabass once and for all as a respected member of the large-orchestra rhythm section. Its advantages over the tuba and sousaphone in handling all manner of tempos—the faster ones in particular—had always been evident; the thing lacking was the sonority, and Pops now achieved that with his slapping technique. The combination of Pops's bass, the driving percussion style of New Orleans drummer Paul Barbarin, and Luis Russell's solid, full-chord comping on piano created an impressive sound and beat.

Unfortunately for Luis Russell, no sooner was the band's personnel solidly established than the Depression began to have serious effects on the music business. Nightclubs folded, dance-hall and theater budgets were cut to the bone, and recording activity ceased for a time. During the period from 1930 to 1935 many musicians were obliged to fall back on vocations not followed for a decade. As the leading jazz bassist in New York, Pops was able to keep going. He was in demand for a variety of engagements: casual gigs around New York, one nighters with pickup bands, short tours with the standby and readily assembled Luis Russell Orchestra, plus the odd record date.

Jazz discographies make no mention of a session with Bessie Smith, but the dates with Jelly Roll Morton and Fats Waller are there; both produced excellent performances. The March 1929 one-shot session with Louis Armstrong produced two titles, including "Mahogany Hall Stomp," Pops's own favorite recording. Several fine sides were made under the nominal leadership of Henry Red Allen, including "Swing Out" and "Feeling Drowsy," which give the measure of the 1929 Luis Russell Orchestra just after Pops joined. The Jelly Roll Morton session was actually a Luis Russell group with Morton replacing the leader on piano. "Hello, Lola" and "One Hour," with Coleman Hawkins and Pee Wee Russell, were made in 1929 with the Mound City Blue Blowers, and those recordings have long enjoyed a reputation among collectors as outstanding small-band jazz performances. The Fats Waller session, also in 1929, brought together a diverse and exciting group of jazz talents: Pops; Fats; dynamic Fletcher Henderson drummer Kaiser Marshall; Red Allen, Albert Nicholas, and J.C. Higginbotham from the Luis Russell ranks; and Jack Teagarden, the distinguished white trombonist from Texas.

—Ross Russell

Chapter 9

New York and the Depression

"When you'd go to work on the train it would be loaded with people, and when you'd come back in the morning there'd be nothing but musicians on it."

꧁꧂

I left for New York on February 11, 1929, and arrived there February 12, 1929. That night I played a dance with Luis Russell's band at the Savoy Ballroom. Benny Carter's band was at the Savoy too. We'd play a half hour and they'd play a half hour. Louis Armstrong was next door with Cal Dixon's band, but we drew all the crowd. We really had a romping band. The union let me in right away because I was the only one around playing my style of string bass, and a lot of guys wanted me. Luis Russell's theme was "Call of the Freaks." We called Luis Russell by his nickname "Fess," for professor. Most of the guys in all the bands called their leader "Fess." I used to call Luis "Toilet," but he'd get salty about it and I cut it out. That's the same name the Ory Band had for Johnny Dodds in New Orleans.

The big music field was Chicago from 1920 to 1925. From 1925, it was in New York. In New York you had a whole bunch of dance halls that had 15- to 18-piece bands. Then all the dancing schools would have six- or seven-piece bands. There were a million nickel dance halls that all had bands. When you'd go to work on the train it would be loaded with people, and when you'd come back in the morning there'd be nothing but musicians on it. With all that music and dancing, it seems like I would have learned to dance. I never did; all I do is get on the floor and wiggle or run and jump.

Fess Williams was the regular house band at the Savoy Ballroom. After Benny Carter finished, Fess came back in as the other band alternating with our band. We were romping so good that Fess used to come over and ask us to play a waltz so his band wouldn't look so bad. Fess wore a high hat with rhinestones and diamonds all over it. He also wore a white tuxedo, and the other guys in his band wore black ones. His playing reminds me of [Mezz] Mezzrow's—just *toot-toot-toot*. I didn't like his band or his clarinet playing. He tried to be funny, but he sure wasn't funny to me.

We played the Savoy Ballroom from February 1929 into the summer. Then we went to the Roseland Ballroom and took Fletcher Henderson's job away from him. We were really romping then, really bouncing. The rhythm was playing great together, and the trumpet players were screaming soft so you could hear the people's feet scraping on the floor. You could stand right in front of the band and they weren't blasting you out. We had Red Allen, J. C. Higginbotham, Paul Barbarin, Albert Nicholas, Charlie Holmes, Teddy Hill, and a whole bunch of great guys. We worked seven days a week and we loved it. We'd rather be working than be at home. It was like it was back in New Orleans. Back then I used to sit around wishing I could go to work. It was a pleasure to work in those days. Russell's band was romping so good in '29 we had everything sewed up around New York. We were playing the same style we played back in early New Orleans.

Some of the guys in New York used to call us the rehearsal band because we rehearsed a lot. But you've got to rehearse to get things together no matter what kind of band you've got. We used to have separate rehearsals for the saxes, the trumpets, the brass, the reeds, and the rhythm. I had to make them all to pick out the rhythm. By the time we played a show, I knew the music so good I never looked at it. Even when you rehearse, you've still got to play with guys awhile before you know what they're going to do. A lot of the bands were just screaming bands; they're not really doing nothin' but screaming. Most of the white bands think if you're not blowing loud, you're not playing nothing. None of them want to study tonation, they just want to blow.

While we were at the Roseland Ballroom we split the bill with Milt Shaw's band out of Detroit. They played half an hour, then we played half an hour. George Raft used to come down there and dance the tango. He was the chauffeur for Arnie Madden, the gangster. We were at the Roseland for about three or four months, and then we went to the Saratoga Club.

Wilbur de Paris was in the Saratoga Club when we went there, and we took his job. We stayed there from late 1929 to about the end of 1931 when the Depression set in. Rex Stewart was with us awhile after he left Fletcher Henderson. Rex was a very good musician and a good guy, but he used to drink a lot of liquor. Another guy who used to play with us was a white kid named Jack Purvis, who came around to sit in. He wanted to play with colored bands so bad he stayed out in the sun for hours getting tanned, and then he'd black his face. During those days from 1929 to 1933 we made a lot of records. I think we recorded under everybody in the band's name except mine.

When we left the Saratoga Club, Luis decided to change his style. We started fooling around with big arrangements and quit romping or playing what you call Dixieland. While we were playing Dixieland we were great. When we started playing like all the other bands, finding work got rough. Why should they hire you when they've already got the same thing?

I met my second wife, Alma, when we both lived in the same apartment house in Harlem on 137th Street in 1931. Her real name is Annie Alma, and before she married me her name was Gayle. During the Depression there was a lot of robbing and murdering going on, so Alma used to get to the apartment house five or ten minutes before I got home from work at the Arcadia Ballroom with Russell's band.

She'd wait until she saw me at the corner, then she'd start in because she figured I'd save her if anything happened.

This waitin' for me and then goin' in went on for a few weeks, and I began to wonder what was up. One night I decided to wait until she went in the door, and then I'd run after her. I really took off, and she thought it was a robber after her so she took off. When I caught her she was nearly scared to death. We talked a lot after that. I'd borrow clothespins and recipes. Finally in 1936 after I was on the road with Armstrong, we decided to get married. We got married at City Hall with Louis and Alpha as our witnesses and the next day I took off on the road again.

After we were married Alma turned Catholic, and we were married in the Catholic church. Now she's a lot stricter about religion than I am. At Lent she gives up something she likes. I give up what I can't get. If people ask me at Lent what I've given up, I tell them, "all the things I can't get." Alma and me never had any kids, but we really love them. I don't think there's anything kids can do to worry us. We love to be with them. Talk to them and play with them.

We had a lot of funny arrangers and songwriters around New York. One white cat that used to write a lot of numbers for McKinney's Cotton Pickers used to get drunk and go sit in the middle of the pond in Central Park on a box to write numbers and arrange tunes. He was very good and came up with some nice numbers. He was a piano player out of Philly. When he'd have a number to sell he'd come around to where the band was rehearsing with his good-looking girl-friend. She'd sit so Luis could see a lot of leg up her dress while the guy would sell Luis the tune. Then they'd leave. This guy had hair so long you couldn't see his face, and he lived down in the Village. He made a very nice arrangement for Armstrong on "Shoe Shine Boy."

Arrangers are really funny guys. Some of them write music you can't read or play. They put notes so you can't tell whether it's on the line or under the line. You've got to guess what the notes are from the first to the last. Some guys write music so hard the musicians can't play it, then they laugh at them. I remember when Bingie Madison wrote some music for Russell's band nobody in the band could play. Somebody got an idea of how to fix him. When Bingie came around next time, the guys asked him to come up and play the tenor sax parts he wrote so we could see how they go. He got up and tried, but they were so hard he couldn't play them himself.

There was a band around New York called the Savoy Sultans, and they got a job playing the whole summer in Atlantic City. They wanted to get some numbers to play, so they got Claude Harper to arrange some music for them. Claude arranged the music so hard for them they couldn't play it, and they lost the job. Then Claude stepped in and took the job for the summer. There was a white boy named Bob Sylvester we used to hire to copy arrangements of other bands down. He could copy down any arrangement he heard once. You had to be careful with him, though; if you were rehearsing a number he'd come around and hear it. Then you'd hear someone else play it before you did. Bob was a kick. He played nice saxophone too. Red Nichols used to come into places where you were playing and sit there all night picking up ideas. You'd hear him later doing the same thing you did.

Another thing that's a kick is to play with a band you're not used to. After 1931 things were rough, and we only played with Luis Russell when he had work. Otherwise we jobbed around. I played with Duke sometimes this way. The first time I played with him, Duke's boys started pulling out the hard stuff to play. I was wise to it and said, "No, man, let's play some of this stuff," and I reached way down at the bottom of the music and pulled out stuff I knew they never played either. The guys who were trying to kid me started saying, "No, man, we never played that stuff." Duke, Cootie [Williams], and some of the guys started laughing at the guys who were making the joke. Duke's band could play real good, but they couldn't read very fast. Every day they'd go to rehearsals and rehearsed just like Russell's band in different sections, then all together. If you work with Duke's band you've got to memorize. They don't hardly play from music at all. Sometimes they just write a few notes down that are hard to remember. Guys like [Johnny] Hodges and [Harry] Carney don't use any music at all—they got memories like elephants. Most of the gigs I worked with Duke were around Philadelphia.

Joe Oliver is the one who made Duke so big. After Joe went to Chicago, he got too big and started wanting too much money for himself. When they opened the Cotton Club in New York, they sent for Joe. Joe was working for the gangsters at the Plantation in Chicago, and he wanted so much money to go the New York boys wouldn't hire him. They put Duke in there instead and that made him. After that Joe had a lot of trouble getting jobs because of the money he wanted.

I gigged some with Fletcher and Horace Henderson's band then. Usually it was with Joe Steele, Horace, and Joe Smith. Joe Smith was one of the best trumpet players around New York; he had a good style. Horace was a very good piano player, I think he plays more piano than Fletcher.

After we left the Saratoga Club we played a lot of different gigs. One of the first jobs was backing Armstrong for two weeks. After that we turned the band over to Cab Calloway for ten weeks. We played three weeks in Philly, two weeks in Washington, D.C., and two weeks in Baltimore. Then we played two weeks at the Apollo Theater for Cab, and then two weeks as the Luis Russell Band. Cab's regular band, the Missourians, were playing the Cotton Club, and he had two sets of dates. After that we did about a three-month run at the Arcadia Ballroom.

When Prohibition came in the gangsters kept getting more and more powerful. Around New York and Chicago "The Boys" pretty much told you where you were gonna work. The union didn't say nothin'. There were a lot of punks around too, we called them the "rat gangsters." We played a dance for them in the early thirties and when we finished they didn't want to pay us. We all got mad and started fighting them. It turned into a battle royal. I got knocked on the head with a chain and got all bloodied up. They took me to the hospital and fixed me. When they finished I tried to get charity treatment, but they saw a diamond ring I had on and made me pay.

There was a guy who lived in Asbury Park named Dupree that booked bands all through the South. We started going on the road more and more in those days. Dupree had an act of his own—singing chickens. When he'd give different signals they would make a noise for him. It was pretty good, and it took a long time to train the chickens. When he was on the road with us once, a guy around the corner from where he was staying stole his chickens. He caught the guy and got him and the chickens before the judge. The judge asked him how he could tell his chickens. He said, "They'll sing when I tell them to." Then he had them sing. The guy who stole them had already eaten one of them. The judge sent him to jail for a while.

One night when we were down South the bus broke down in a swampy area. Otis Johnson, the trumpet player, and I took off out in the swamp looking for a snake while they fixed the bus. We found one and killed it, then we walked about two miles to a store to get some string. We tied the string on the neck of the snake and propped its head up with a stick. When we got back on the bus we hid it in the front and carried the string to the back of the bus. Finally they got the bus ready to go, and the driver turned the lights on and had everybody stick their heads out in the aisle so we could see if everybody was there. We started pulling the snake down the aisle then. Everybody went wild—guys jumped out of the windows and climbed in the luggage racks and everything. It was a kick.

During the rough times in the Depression we thought of a lot of little ways to make some money. When Marcus Garvey was around New York he put on big affairs at the ball park and wanted me to play them for nothin'. I said, "No, man, I can't eat on nothin'." Then this guy told me it was a nice deal, and after you played you could walk up through the crowd and pass the hat. So I tried it. I played, then I passed my hat as I went on up the stairs. When I got to the gate I had about seven dollars, and I just kept going. It was a nice touch but I got too many guys doing it. They caught one guy and put him in jail for 30 days, and that killed it.

Bob White from New Orleans and I got another thing going on the numbers. All the colored people all over thought everybody from New Orleans knew voodoo and could work great things for them. Bob and I bought ten cents' worth of incense and some envelopes, got a frog, a green rag, and a table and chair. We set up the table and chair on the corner with a bunch of envelopes with numbers in them. Bob wrapped the green rag around his head like a turban. We put a sign on the table, "Lucky Numbers." When somebody would want a lucky number, Bob would hold the frog and say some French, then let him jump on one of the envelopes. I'd burn a little incense under the envelope and we'd sell it to the guy for a quarter. Then we'd give it to him and say, "Don't forget us when you win." We had to pay the cop on the beat two dollars a week to keep the table there, but he took his payoff in lucky numbers.

Around this time I had one of the best jobs I ever had. It was a little four-piece string band of Joe Venuti, Eddie Lang, Dick McDonough, and me that played on the radio. A violin, two guitars, and string bass. It was beautiful—even at rehearsals people crowded around to hear us. It was so good I knew it wasn't going to last. Man, we were really doing some stuff. Joe sure could play violin; he was really good. Eddie played guitar just like you play piano. He knew the chords and his instrument. Eddie was about the best guitar player around. Dick was very good too. Eddie and Dick were the only white guitar players I knew up to that time. The radio program folded after a couple of weeks.

At 131st Street and Seventh Avenue there was a place called the Band Box where all the guys used to go to have battles. The owner had piano, drums, and bass. Then other guys would come in with their in-struments like sax, clarinet, trumpet, trombone, and what have you, trying to cut each other. We'd usually go there in the morning after work. I usually didn't stick around. It was just one room with guys all packed in. Luckey Roberts, James P., Fats, Teddy Wilson, and all the piano players used to come around. Jelly would come in the evening sometimes, but he'd hang around the corner outside talking to his gang. They would all be listening to Jelly. As long as you stood there and laughed and agreed, he'd talk all day. Nothing he said sounded right to me.

Jelly had some good men on his records, and he had a guy who did the arrangements for him. Jelly would say the music goes something like this and the guy would write it down. Then the guy would say, "What do you want going in the first chorus, what do you want in the second," and so on. It was like having a guy write a book and you telling him what to put in it. They'd figure out the changes, the first ending, the second ending, and the coda. Jelly played some tough tunes, like "King Porter Stomp" and "The Pearls." A lot of bands won't play them because they're too tough; they have too many changes.

Bill "Bojangles" Robinson and Wellman Braud were like Jelly; they'd talk as long as anyone would listen and hung around outside the Band Box. After Braud got written up in *Ripley's Believe It or Not* column, he was too big for anybody. Ripley said he could pick faster than any bass player. He quit Duke's band and started one of his own. He got a nice little band together to play a place over in Jersey. He talked so much to the man who owned the place about where to put the tables and how things were in the wrong place, the man told him to get his band together and get the hell outta there. He was always talking him-self in by showing the clipping from the column, and then he'd talk himself right out again.

I know Braud couldn't pick as fast as I could, and I never saw any-one else who could. A couple of guys were better at playing melody than me—Jimmy Blanton and Junior Raglin. They could both play a whole lot of melody but had trouble keeping a rhythm foundation. Raglin was a guitar player and Blanton was a cello player before they switched to bass. Blanton played string bass like he played the cello.

A lot of guys who'd come to New York heard about the Band Box, and they would come in there with their horns when they hit town, wanting to battle with the guys. We'd get one of the hotshots like Coleman Hawkins or Chu Berry to come down, and they'd go at it. Albert Morgan, Sam's brother, hit town from New Orleans one day and started shooting his head off about how he could play bass. The guys came and got me out of bed to come down for a little cutting contest. When he saw me come in he told everybody he knew me in New Orleans and I was his friend and he wouldn't play against me. I went along and said, "No, I won't play against Morgan, he's my friend," and I wanted to see him get some work around there. He was a very nice kid.

I usually hung out at the Rhythm Club, where the musicians got together to play poker and gamble. At three or four in the afternoon you could find nearly every musician in town there. You could catch a gig there for the night or a recording date for later on. Lester Lanin used to have six or seven bands going around New York, and he'd come there and hire you for Jewish, Italian, or any kind of music. I played a lot of different gigs like that for him. The old musicians around New York used to hang out at the Amsterdam Club. You had your own key and went right on in. Mostly the guys gambled there. I met Scott Joplin's nephew in there about 1929. I just shook his hand and said hello.

I never had much to do with a lot of guys around New York. Coleman Hawkins was one; he was on a different kick than we were. He was also a sometimes guy—sometimes he'd look right at you and didn't know you, and sometimes he did. After a while I started doing the same thing to him. Tommy Ladnier was the same way. One night he'd come in and look at me, then walk right on by like he didn't know me.

The next night he'd come in and say, "Hello, George Foster, I saw you last night." I'd say, "I know you did, you looked right at me. How did you recognize me tonight?" It used to make me mad, and if I wanted to get him, I'd say, "Tommy, you been knowin' me ever since Biloxi." He'd say, "Aw, man, let's not get into that." I'd say, "Don't go into what? Biloxi's your home, ain't it?" He'd get hot and walk away. He didn't claim Biloxi; he wanted everyone to think he was from New Orleans. Tommy was a very fine trumpet player.

Some bandleaders when they have trouble with a guy or with the union will call the whole band together. Luis Russell used to do that a lot. He'd be having trouble with a guy and would talk to all of us about the trouble. When times were rough and we were chargin' less than union scale, Luis would get in trouble with the union. He'd call us together and say, "We got trouble with the union." I'd say, "Man, we ain't got no trouble, you got trouble." Then he'd say, "We got to go before the union board." Someone would say, "We don't gotta go before no board." Earl Hines was another leader that way. He used to have a lot of trouble with Muggsy Spanier and Darnell Howard. He'd call us together and get goin' about the problem when someone would pipe up and say, "What did you call all of us down here for when you want to talk to Darnell?" And he'd say, "I'm gonna do that right now."

Wilton Crawley was a character. The way he played clarinet was standing on his head. He'd keep screwing around in a circle while he was playing. That was part of his act on the stage. When we were cutting records for Victor, Crawley wanted to stand on his hand to record. Mr. Watson of Victor said no. Crawley was just nuts. He played clarinet like Ted Lewis, not too good.

There were two Jabbo Smiths that I knew. One was the famous one from around Chicago and New York. He could play trumpet and trombone very good. He drank a lot and got in trouble. He was in

Joliet [prison] for a while. Most of the time he was in and out of jail. The other Jabbo also played trumpet and was from around Boston. He was very bad too, maybe worse than the famous Jabbo. He'd fight, get cut up, drink, and get in trouble.

Shows are the hardest thing to play, especially for toe dances. They're counting beats all the time, and the musicians got to be following the music very close. The drummer has got to read and be very good because he hits the drums on catches and jumps. If he misses, the whole thing looks silly. A lot of leaders, like Cab Calloway and Noble Sissle, couldn't even wave their sticks for it. They were guys who were singers or had some kind of reputation. When they rehearsed, the piano player, or the real leader, would lead the band, and he'd show the stick-waver how to get them started and stopped. Noble Sissle had a pretty good ear for this. They let them in the musician's union even though they couldn't play a note, and Noble Sissle even ran for president of the union in New York and lost. Tiny Bradshaw and Lucky Millinder were another couple of these guys. They could play a little honky-tonk drums and led bands. As soon as the bands broke up on those guys, they went right out of the music business.

I played some shows and made some records with Bessie Smith in New York. After the shows I used to go to her dressing room, eat candy, and talk a lot of trash. She was nice, very nice. She knew what she was doing and she was my favorite blues singer. All of the big stars, like Bessie, Clara Smith, Snakehips, Stepin Fetchit, were so easy to get along with. It was the little stars that just came up and the mediocre stars and chorus dancers that were the hardest to get along with. They didn't know the music and couldn't get it. They would scream and be nasty to the musicians and try to blame everything that went wrong on them.

In New York going to a recording session was like going on a picnic. The most fun was with Fats Waller. He'd pack up a suitcase like he was going on a trip, but it would be full of whiskey. When he'd get to the recording studio he'd pass bottles out to the guys. Then Fats would sit at the piano with his bottle and a big glass to drink out of. Him and James P. Johnson would sit down and fool around on the piano. They'd write and arrange the number right there in the studio. Then Fats would say something like, "Let's time this chorus." He'd have them time one chorus of what he was doing. As fast as Fats would play it, Jimmy would write it out. When Fats finished he'd go get a drink. Jimmy would write the music out and pass it around to the guys. Sometimes if Jimmy needed a note, he'd go over to the piano and find it. Fats would sit down and say, "Okay, fellas; B-flat we're gonna do this in." And off we'd go.

I never did know what tunes I made with Fats. The music just had numbers on them, like 1A, 2A, 4B. Fats would say 4B and we'd play it. When the number came out on record it had a name, but we didn't know nothin' about it. I didn't make too many records with Fats because he was very tough to get your money from. You never got paid until you caught him, then he'd usually only give you a piece of what he owed you.

James P. Johnson was the nicest guy you ever will meet. He was well spoken and so kind. I used to love to stand around and hear Jimmy talk. When he came to the West Coast about 1941 or 1942, he couldn't get along with Albert Nicholas. It was Albert Nicholas's fault because you couldn't hardly find anything to get mad at James P. about. Jimmy always talked very soft and tried to help guys with their music. Jimmy would tell you when you were wrong. Then he would tell you when you were right.

Jimmy always wanted someone to come to the studio with him when he cut piano rolls or made records just to have some company. He'd want you to go out and get his booze, and you'd sit and drink and joke. He used to come to the house and get me when he was going to the studio. I used to go so I could look out the top floor where the studio was and see the girls sunbathin' naked on the roof tops. The girls would wave and say, "Hello, there, fellas." The studio was at 113 57th Street. The only person around the studio was the recording controller, and he didn't mind all the stuff goin' on. Sometimes Jimmy would bring four or five people with him.

Jimmy made a lot of player piano rolls. The first time I saw him recording rolls I thought he'd blowed his top. He was playing a regular piano, but no sound was coming out. I asked him what he was doing. He stopped, ran the roll back and played it for me. You play the piano just like a regular one, but every time you hit it, it punches a hole.

Jimmy could write music very fast. He's the fastest one I know of. If you told him to arrange something, when you finish playing he'll sit down at the piano and play it and say, "This what you want?" Then he'd write it out. Bingie Madison was very fast too. If he heard an arrangement twice, he could write it out on his shirt cuffs. Jimmy wrote good so you could read it when he finished; they weren't just scratches. Joe Steele went to the conservatory, and you couldn't read nothin' he wrote.

James P. was a much better piano player than Jelly. Jelly was a good entertaining piano player, but he wasn't in the same league with James P. or Fats.

I didn't record with Jimmy until way later, right before he died. I'd been knowing him for a long time though. He used to stay at our house a lot. He would be rehearsing one of those big shows or something like that and wouldn't get through till way late. He'd come by our house, and I wouldn't let him go all the way out to Long Island. Sometimes he'd have Duke or someone else with him, and they'd stay too. We'd usually call Lil and let her know where he was. Sometimes she'd come to town and stay at our place with him. We used to go out to Jimmy's place and play a lot too. Jimmy never talked much except about music. He was always writing it, playing it, and talking about it. He taught Fats how to play. They lived right across from each other on Long Island, and Clarence Williams lived right there too. Jimmy was a very fine musician.

Willie the Lion Smith used to live in the same apartment house I did in Harlem. Willie is what you call a born musician. He was a very slow reader and couldn't play in the big bands but was very good with the small ones. Willie could play in more keys than anyone except James P.

Willie and I used to play with Leadbelly. I think we were the only two guys who could play with him. Leadbelly didn't know which key he was going to play in. He'd play in all naturals and sharps. We'd have to listen to him then, search around to find the key. Then when we found it, we'd take off. Josh White and most of them guitar players weren't good musicians. They just play the blues. When Willie and I would play with them kinda guys, he'd come around to say, "We got a hard date today, Pops." A lot of those guys can't even tune their instruments.

Leadbelly didn't know when to start or stop. The recording companies always had to go and splice his endings on. Leadbelly's wife's name was Irene, and the tune of his "Irene" got to be a big hit. As soon as it did he died. Leadbelly was a mean and evil guy. He was in the penitentiary three times for killing guys, and every time he played his way out. I was at his house one day with one of the partners of Asch Records talking about making some records, when he nearly killed a guy. Leadbelly's son-in-law insulted this guy's wife, and he chased the son-in-law up to Leadbelly's door. They were fighting in the doorway when Leadbelly picked up an iron poker and started hitting the guy in the head with it. Me and the guy from Asch got out of the place and took off. When Leadbelly went before the judge for beating the guy we had to go to court with him. The judge knew about Leadbelly's singing and that he was on parole, and he didn't want to send him back to jail. So he told the guy he nearly killed that he had no business in Leadbelly's house and fined him, and withdrew the charges against Leadbelly.

When Leadbelly would get mad he'd just sit and grit his teeth. One time I told him he'd have to play a chord up on his guitar or we couldn't make no record. He just sat and started gritting his teeth. I told him he could grit his teeth all day, but if he didn't play the chord we couldn't play with him. He finally played it. Another time the government told him he had to pay taxes, and he was mad because he'd never paid before. He just sat and gritted his teeth; I told him to have the man take it out before he got paid. Leadbelly was just a mean and evil man. I just made records with him and never hung around with him at all.

Willie the Lion was always getting a band up for rehearsal and no job showed up. In the Depression this was okay because we wasn't doin' nothin' anyway. One time after I married Alma we were getting ready to go to her home in South Carolina for a visit. I had my clothes all packed and sent to have them put on the train. Willie came around and said we had a job starting the next day. I stayed, turned in my ticket, and didn't have no clothes until Alma got back. That job ain't come up yet.

Perry Bradford was from Memphis. He wrote a whole lot of blues. He was one of those old honky-tonk piano players that played with one finger. I got to know him some around New York. He played like George Thomas, Udell Wilson, and Manny Johns and his wife. Manny Johns and his wife were the only man-and-wife team I know of that played around New Orleans. One would sing and one would play the piano. If it go so they weren't making any tips, they'd switch off. In New Orleans most piano players made their money working in the whorehouses, but around Chicago and New York they made most of their money at house rent parties or what we called fish fries in New Orleans. In Chicago and New York they'd serve chitlins, pigs' feet, and gin. Sometimes they'd call them "birthday parties." You'd get an invitation to a birthday party, and when you got there you had to pay to get in and then buy your own food and booze. Guys like Bradford, Jimmy Yancey, and Luckey Roberts used to make good money playing those affairs. They also played the tonks. Along State Street in Chicago there used to be a whole lot of them. Luckey Roberts was a fine piano player. I played a couple of shows with him. He was a little bitty guy but he was very strong. One night a couple of guys tried to hold him up. He

grabbed them and knocked their heads together and then started whip-
ping them something awful. By the time the police arrived the two rob-
bers were hollering for the cops Luckey was beating them up so bad.
Luckey used to do all the big piano jobs around New York.

I played with Teddy Wilson at the French Casino in New York.
That was the old Earl Carroll Theatre at 51st Street and Seventh Avenue. Upstairs they had a bar where Teddy and I played. Downstairs
they had two bands, one that played the shows and Noble Sissle's that
played the dances. Teddy was a very quiet guy and very nice. About all
he'd ever say was, "Hello, how're you doin'?" Teddy was a very good
piano player and had a different style of playing than the other players. He played very good with a band or all by himself. He played all
over the piano. He wasn't as good as Art Tatum. Tatum was out there
all by himself, but he was a liquor head. Even that didn't stop Tatum.
He was so good he could walk out of a place or get fired and walk right
into another place and the people would be glad to have him, juice
head and all. He was a genius. If you're playing with him and he takes
a solo, you can't play for listening to him.

The arrangement that rejoined Louis Armstrong, then the biggest name in jazz, with Pops and other former New Orleans comrades came about as the result of booking-agency maneuvers. In 1935 Armstrong signed a personal management contract with the aggressive and astute Joe Glaser of Chicago. Glaser's first move was to refurbish the Armstrong orchestral image, somewhat tarnished by a succession of weak accompanying orchestras. Louis had not recorded since January 1933, except for an unimportant session made in Paris with a European pickup group. The new team—Louis backed by the settled, sonorous, and powerful Luis Russell Orchestra—began auspiciously with a series of record sessions in New York starting in October 1935 for the new Decca label, a 35-cent seller that was moving aggressively into jazz and pop.

Emphasizing standard and current material—"La Cucaracha," "On Treasure Island," "Red Sails in the Sunset," "You Are My Lucky Star"—and trimmed to less than three minutes to meet jukebox demands, the recordings were dominated by Armstrong's vocals and high-note trumpet playing. (Louis had long since ceased to play cornet.) Besides the standard tunes a few interesting originals were recorded, including "Swing That Music," and a new version of a New Orleans favorite, "Mahogany Hall Stomp."

The band was heard to great advantage on tour. There were many of these, long and short, to various parts of the U.S., often with incredible jumps between the one-nighters that Joe Glaser had been able to book, like the one mentioned by Pops, from Bangor, Maine, to New Orleans. Pops's salary of $77 a week was expected to cover maintaining a home for Alma in New York as well as his own expenses while on the road. These trips were always stimulating enough but replete with hardship: lack of accommodations, hasty and missed meals, catnaps in the jolting bus between engagements, and Jim Crow conditions. The chance discovery of Bunk Johnson in New Iberia, Louisiana, in 1937 led to a rehabilitation movement to bring the veteran trumpet player back to the jazz scene, although this did not take place until the war years. Fitted with new teeth, Bunk made a triumphal return to music in San Francisco and later led his own bands in New York. (The LP Bunk Johnson and his Superior Jazz Band contained a long recorded interview with Bunk and interesting examples of re-created New Orleans small-band style.)

The wholesale firing in 1940 of the men in the Louis Armstrong–Luis Russell Orchestra by Joe Glaser was typical of the dubious practices prevalent in the music business. Thereafter Armstrong recorded with various pickup groups—the Mills Brothers and Casa Loma Orchestra among them—before forming a seven-piece combo to play concerts.

Pops Foster began one of the worst periods of his life. His fortunes did not improve until after the war. He appeared on the radio show This Is Jazz, produced by jazz authority Rudi Blesh, made a successful tour of Europe with Mezz Mezzrow in 1948, and recorded for Mezzrow's King Jazz label. Then he returned to the West Coast to join Earl Hines for a long, steady, and artistically rewarding stay at the Club Hangover in San Francisco. That was in 1955. Thereafter Pops made San Francisco his home and worked there almost continually with small bands playing in the authentic prewar style until his death in 1969.

—Ross Russell

Chapter 10

Traveling with Armstrong and After

"Sometimes you have it good in life and sometimes rough."

꧁꧂

ouis Armstrong tried all of the bands around New York, but none
of them would give up their name permanently for him. In 1935
Luis Russell gave up our name to Armstrong, and we were known as
Louis Armstrong's band after that. Before that, Louis had used our
band a lot of times for recording dates and different gigs, but we always went back to Luis Russell's name. I was with Armstrong from
1935 until I got fired in 1940.

We worked a lot more under Russell than we did under Armstrong.
When we went with Armstrong we were all real glad and thought we'd
make a lot more money. But Joe Glaser, his manager, wanted a lot of
money for Louis. He wanted guarantees, advances, and a percentage.
People just didn't have a lot of money in those days, and they wouldn't
come out enough to afford big prices. So we didn't get as many dates.
I was making 77 dollars a week when we worked. When we made it,
we spent it. Before I got married I gambled a lot and drank some.
When you hit a new town everybody was glad to see you because they
knew you spent a lot of money. I'd gamble on anything—poker, black-
jack, tonk, fantan, craps, or anything else. If Joe Glaser didn't have any

work, we'd loaf. We didn't get any pay, but Joe would loan us money.
After I married Alma she'd send me money to live on so I wouldn't owe
Joe everything when we got to working.

One time in 1937 we were loafing in Chicago and I was playing
gigs with some outlaw guys on the South Side. I'd seen some of Benny
Goodman's boys around town. Benny had a recording date and they
couldn't find [bassist] Harry Goodman, so they went out to get me.
When they got me and got back, I got there about the same time
Harry did, so we both played on the records.

The guys in the band sure were glad I was getting a little work because they were all broke and I'd share what I had with them. We all
shared when we were broke, except Louis Bacon. Louis Bacon had
money, and he never asked nobody for nothing and he never gave
nothing. When I got sick with pneumonia all the guys gave some
money to help except him. He said, "I'm not giving those New Orleans
cat nothin'." When he got sick in New Orleans, I was the only one in
the band that went to the hospital to see him. I carried some soup up
to him that Alma made. He sat up in the bed and cried.

With Armstrong we traveled a whole lot. Once we jumped from Bangor, Maine, to New Orleans for a one-nighter, then on to Houston,
Texas, for the next night. Traveling never worried me like it did the
other guys. We'd take off and they'd start saying how far we had to go.
I knew how far it was, so there wasn't any point thinking about it. Armstrong always traveled by bus because it would take you right to where
you were going. Some of the bands like Duke's and Cab's traveled by
train, but they were always switching connections and taking cabs to
hotels and so on.

It was tough traveling through the South in those days. We had two
white guys with us—the bus driver and Joe Glaser. If you had a colored
bus driver back then, they'd lock him up in every little country town for
"speeding." It was very rough finding a place to sleep in the South. You
couldn't get into the hotel for whites, and the colored didn't have any
hotels. You rented places in private homes, boardinghouses, and whore-

houses. The food was awful, and we tried to find places where we could cook. We carried a bunch of pots and pans around with us.

Charlie Holmes and I palled around together, and we always found some way to have a good time. The rest of the guys were always watching to see what we cooked up. One time the two of us were broke in Texas and wanted to have a drink. We decided to get Bobby Austin, who was the vocalist with the band and was Sonny Woods's girlfriend. When we'd travel they'd fight all the time. He'd knock her down, she'd lay there for a while, then get up and hit him with a shoe or something, then he'd knock her down again. We always had to move our card game to keep out of their fights. We started telling Bobby how bad Sonny was and how awful he treated her. Every time we'd come up with something else: "It's a shame how bad Sonny treats you; you're so good to him and he's such a bum." She'd say, "Have another drink, boys." We had a nice little thing going there for a while until Sonny caught us. He got real hot.

One time we were stuck in Tulsa, Oklahoma, and hadn't had any work for about a month. Sonny Woods, Midge Williams, and myself got a crap game going. Midge had gotten to know the local sheriff, and he gave us protection. We'd get a few guys to play with Midge at one end in a very low-cut dress and Sonny or me at the other end. When Midge would shoot she'd bend real low so everybody could see her titties. All the guys would be looking them, and we'd call whatever number we wanted and pick up the dice. We got enough money to get us to Kansas City and then Memphis for a week's work.

I never fooled around with none of the showgirls we worked with. To me they were just like a bunch of horses. I just never paid them any mind. Sometimes I'd hustle a bottle to introduce some guy to one of them. He'd want to meet one and I'd tell him to bring me a taste and I'd try to fix it up. Then I'd tell the girl and I'd give her a taste. Besides that, when we got off they went one way and I went another. If you want to get along, don't fool with no girls you work with. They expect too much out of you. If you're going on the road they always try to team up with you. They know you're going to pay the rent and they're going to eat. If they'd come around I'd tell them my landlady don't allow no company. Some of the guys fooled around with them. Most of the guys were looking for a place to sleep and eat for nothin', just like the girls. I used to gamble with the girls sometimes and beat them out of their money.

When two bands would meet on the road, we'd all get together and make a whole gang of noise and get thrown out of hotels. In 1936 our band, the Isham Jones Band, and the Benson Band all met in Iowa, and all three bands got thrown out in the street for cuttin' up.

When I was on the road with Armstrong and we'd get close to New York, I'd call Alma and she'd meet me, like in Chicago, and we'd stay together there for a week or so. Sometimes when the band would take off she'd go with me for a month or two, and sometimes she'd just go on back to New York. Alma is my second wife and the best thing I ever locked up on. I always say the reason I lived so long isn't because I took care of myself, because I didn't. The reason is, I locked up on a good wife. I never was what you call a corner bum, though. Those are guys that stand around a certain street corner all day or hang around a saloon. Even if I went gambling I'd take ten dollars with me, or whatever I was going to play with, and if I'd lose I'd take off. I couldn't stand to just hang around swallowing bets like some of the guys. Some of them would play your hand harder than you did. Most musicians don't eat right and don't even go home at night. It kills them off.

Louis's second wife, Lil, sure was good to him. She still loves him after all these years. The reason she took off was Louis's pot smoking. There wasn't any woman or nothin'; she just got tired of Louis smoking that stuff. He smoked pot just like you smoke regular cigarettes. The band was playing Jack Sheen's in New Orleans when she left. Jack's was a wide-open space in St. Bernard's Parish. Louis smoked pot all the time I was with him, and as far as I know never quit.

Louis should give more credit to Lil than anyone for teaching him how to play. She was a great piano player and a great musician. Lil's a nice girl too, not wild or mean at all. Louis should also give a lot of credit to old man Joe Oliver for teaching him how to play tunes and arrangements.

I knew all of Louis's wives. His first wife was a rough gal, Daisey. Daisey used to go with Eddie Atkins, the trombone player, before she married Louis. She used to work all over New Orleans and she used to come down to the Come Clean Hall every Sunday night to dance when I was playing there. She finally went to Chicago, and I never heard no more about her.

Louis's third wife, Alpha, used to travel around with the band before they were married. They lived together for about ten years before they got married, then when they got married it only lasted about four years. When they fought they really went after each other.

I got my nickname from Louis Armstrong. He calls everyone "Pops." The name just stuck on me. In New Orleans some of the guys called me "the Fireman" or "Fireman George." We used to call Louis "Poppa."

Louis was always a happy-go-lucky guy about most things. I've seen him do a lot of crazy things, like start on stage without any pants on. I remember one time a guy hit Louis for a handout. Louis gave him a quarter and the guy said, "Hey man, don't put me down like that!" Louis said, "Okay man, let's have it back!" The guy did, thinking Louis was gonna give him more. Louis put the quarter in his pocket and took off.

Louis is real jealous of other players who put out. If you play bad you won't be in the band, and if you play too good you won't be there. When I'd get to romping along on the bass, he'd yell at me, "Hey, man, if you want to play trumpet, come on down here and play." I'd say, "Go on, man, and blow your horn." He's lucky he's lived so long. He works too hard because he don't want nobody to do nothing but him. Louis shouldn't be so jealous, because he's an outstanding man.

❧

I've had a good time in my life playing music and traveling around the world. It's kicks, man! You really learn people. I can look at a guy right now and tell you, "That guy is no good, he's a rat," or "That cat's all right." When I see a guy come up to the stand I can tell you if he's going to start trouble or not. You sure learn a lot from traveling and meeting people.

I remember Bob Smiley, Louis's valet and bodyguard, and how I dealt with him once when he owed me a quarter and wouldn't pay me just to be nasty. We were playing Little Rock, Arkansas, and were headed toward New Orleans. I just started on him from the opposite direction by saying, "Man, I don't want you to pay me, but wait until we get to New Orleans where I can get some dust." Louis Bacon said, "Man, you wouldn't use none of that dust on him would you?" And I said, "Man, you don't know how long he owed me a quarter, but I don't want it now. I'd rather get some dust and turn him into a lizard." Smiley followed me around for a week after that trying to pay me the quarter, and I'd just say, "No, man, I gotta put the dust on you now." Finally, just before we got to New Orleans I took it and gave him a good warning.

We used to pull some bad tricks on Paul Barbarin because he was so afraid of ghosts. Sometimes we'd go in his room to call up spirits or pretend we were talking to ghosts. When we were leaving the hotel in Chicago we stole some sheets one time. That night out on the road we stopped for a break. Paul had been drinking and was about half gassed. A bunch of us put on the sheets across the road from the bus, then one of us hit the side of the bus where Paul was snoozing. He stuck his head up and we started jumping up and down. He took off outta the bus and ran down the road till we couldn't see him. When he came back everybody was laughing and he wanted to fight.

Another time Paul met this girl, and he told her he was in the dress business. He took her up to his room at the Douglas Hotel in Philly. My room was right next to his, and we listened to them. They decided to go get something to drink and then come back. When they got back we had Albert Nicholas under the bed with a fork to scratch on the bed springs and a string tied to one of the chairs we could pull from the next room. We'd look through the keyhole and make sure the girl could see the chair move. She said, "Mr. Barbarin, Mr. Paul, that chair's moving." Paul said, "Don't worry, you're with a man, nothing's going to happen to you!" We pulled the chair again and Nick hit the bed springs with the fork. She wet all over the floor, ran out of the room and took off. Paul took off too. When he came back he came to my room, and there were nine of us guys in there pretending like we were sleeping. He wanted to fight all of us.

From 1910 to 1937 I didn't see Bunk Johnson. In 1910 he left New Orleans with a minstrel show. In 1937 Louis's band was playing a Catholic dance in New Iberia, Louisiana, and I saw Louis talking to this old guy. After we started playing, I said to Louis, "Who's that old guy?"

Louis said, "That's Bunk Johnson."

I said, "I didn't even recognize him."

Louis said, "I didn't either, man."

The next intermission I went over and talked to Bunk for a while. He said he'd been driving sugarcane wagons. He sure had changed in those 27 years. He didn't have no teeth at all. He said he'd been with the minstrel show for a long time. Those minstrel show cars were really funny. They'd hook them on the back of the train and then put them off at the siding of the town where they were going. The show people would mostly live in the car because people wouldn't rent them rooms. Show people would steal anything they could carry and then not pay the rent. They'd steal chickens, rabbits, sheets, clothes, or anything.

After we met Bunk in New Iberia some guys from San Francisco found him and carried him to San Francisco. He played there for quite a while, but he got to drinking and they sent him back to Louisiana. In 1945 Sidney Bechet and I met Bunk in New Orleans and carried him to Boston to play with us. The first night in Boston he got drunk and didn't show up. Alma went out looking for him. When she found him he was drunk and had lost his horn. After that he straightened up for a while. Then Gene Williams wanted him to come to New York. Gene would get him drunk so Sidney would fire him, and it worked.

I've only missed a couple of gigs in my life. In 1937 I missed a movie gig with Armstrong. We were in New York and were going to leave for Hollywood. I was down with a mild case of pneumonia. Luis Russell came to the house and told me, "Pops, we're leaving for L.A. without you." I got worse then and went to the hospital the next day. I nearly died, and it was two months before I caught up with them. Those movie deals were nice; you picked up a nice piece of change on them. When I finally caught up with the band, some of the guys were short of money, and so I asked them what they did with the money from the movie. They said they didn't make no picture. The movie outfit wanted the band to wear blackface and they wouldn't. Cab Calloway's band wouldn't either. They finally got Tommy or Jimmy Dorsey's band and they wore half-masks to make them look black.

In about 1935 or 1936 we started playing for audiences that just sat there. I never liked this; I always like to play for an audience that dances. The kind of music I like to play is the faster stuff where you can really get to romping along. I don't really like to play many blues. They're slow and draggy. Some good ones like Basin Street Blues you can rock along with.

In 1940 Joe Glaser fired the whole band to get a cheaper band. I was making 77 dollars a week when we worked, and some of the guys were only making 66 dollars and doing arrangements too. The reason they told me was I was too old, and Jimmy Archey got told he was too short. Joe hired some of the guys back at a cheaper price. Some of the new guys he hired couldn't play the music, and that was about the end of the band. They went downhill fast after that. Things got really rough for me, too.

Sometimes you have it good in life and sometimes rough. About the roughest time I've had was after I got fired from Armstrong's band. I made some records for a lot of little companies with different small groups and played a few gigs around New York. We were really scuffling to make it, and then I got sick with pneumonia again. The finance company came and took all our furniture. Alma and me finally got my nephew to move us into a little room where he could help take care of us. Things finally started getting a little better, and we wriggled out of it.

It was around this time I went to Chicago and recorded blues for a whole week. Panassié had set up the session so Mezz Mezzrow could record. They didn't put any name on the blues until later. Mezzrow claimed that he composed a lot of them. Panassié thinks that Mezzrow is the greatest. When Mezz is playing, he sits there rocking back and forth like Mezz is outta this world. Any little boy can play the clarinet or sax as good as Mezz can. He just stands up there and goes *toot-toot-toot*. Mezz sure is a good manager, though, and a very nice guy. I like him, but man, he can't play no jazz.

In 1942 things got so bad in music I said I'd rather grab me a broom and start working. I went and took the test for subway work in New York. After the test I had my preference of a porter's job or workin' the change booth. One of the guys told me, "Pops, you'd better not take a job working the change booth because you can't sneak off. The best job around is the porter's, even though it don't pay a nickel, because you can slip off when you want to." I took the porter's job and stayed with it from 1942 to 1945 when I went with Sidney Bechet.

As soon as I started workin' I started slippin' off. I played all over New York and the other little places there are around there; I even slipped off to play gigs in Canada and Washington, D.C. My boss, Mr. Horton, was awful good to me. The most work I did was hiding from the inspector. He'd come by to check if we were there, then get on the train. I'd get on the same train but the next car back. When I'd come back I'd bring Horton a box of those stinky old cheroot cigars.

The water gigs I slipped off to and played in Washington, D.C., were great. They were kind of a symphony sort of thing. They'd take us out on boats to barges tied in the middle of the river, then we'd play for the people back on the bank. You get a different sound from music when you're playing on the water like that. It sure was beautiful.

One night I took off to play a big party in New York. Right in front of me one of the big shots on the subway, Mr. Bagley, sat down. He kept looking at me, and I kept looking like I never saw him. The next

day though the word came down for me to go to his office. When I got
there, he said, "Why didn't you ever tell me you played music."

I said, "Who told you?"

He said "I saw you."

I said, "Where?"

He said, "Last night—I kept passing you music to play all night
on a little slip of paper. Don't you remember?" I said, "Oh, yeah, it was
you!" Then he said I did a nice job and told me if I had to take off
again just to tell the inspector he'd okayed it.

I used to play Minton's in New York before Dizzy Gillespie and
Charlie Parker worked there. I was fronting a little group when Teddy
Hill took over the management. Teddy was sore at me then, and so he
fired my band. I played with Diz and Charlie; both of them were great.
Diz could do all that crazy stuff on his horn, and then stop and play
a whole lot of trumpet. He'd do more crazy stuff on his horn than anybody. Diz and Charlie started all that stuff they're doing today. It was
a symphony kind of music. Those two guys didn't overdo it, and they
were the best that played that kind of music. Charlie used to drink a
lot, but I never saw him take dope. Diz always loves to get me to sit
and talk to him about the old times.

I took a vacation down to New Orleans in 1943 and met Sidney
Bechet on Perdido and Rampart. He came up to me and said, "What
you doin' around here, old man?"

I said, "What do you mean, dad?" While we were there we got
some guys together and made some records for the USO at the Mai-
son Blanche building. We got Louis Keppard, Alphonse Picou, Big
Eye Louis Nelson, Peter Bocage, a guy named Henry on trombone,
and a guy named Valcons on piano. We sure made a lot of music, but
none of us ever heard the records. Sidney asked me if I wanted to play
with his band he was gonna get for a Boston date he had. He said he
was gonna get Bunk Johnson, so I said I'd do it too.

Before I left New Orleans I had a couple of sets of strings for my
bass that were too tight for my instrument, but I thought they were

just right for Slow Drag Pavageau's. I hadn't seen Slow Drag, so I gave them to Jim Robinson, the trombone player, to give to him. A few years later I was back in New Orleans and I met Slow Drag. I asked him how he liked the strings I'd sent to him. I also told him I was kind of mad he hadn't written and thanked me. He said, "I don't know, man. I never got them. Who'd you give them to?"

I said, "Jim Robinson."

Slow Drag said, "That dirty bastard—he sold them to me!" They didn't speak for a couple of years after that.

I went back to New York and took a six-month leave of absence to go play with Sidney's band. From the time we opened we had trouble with Bunk, but I've already talked about it. Sidney fired Bunk and sent to New Orleans for Peter Bocage. He came and started telling everybody how to play, so Sidney fired him and got a kid named Johnny Windhurst to finish the job with us.

Some of the problems we had may have been Sidney's fault. He is the most selfish, hard-to-get-along-with guy I ever worked with. I saw him fire one trumpet player five times in one night. You really had to try to get along with him. From the time I played with him in Jack Carey's band in New Orleans to making a bunch of Blue Note records with him, he was a tough baby and all for himself.

After the Boston job gave out I went back to New York and worked around with Art Hodes in the Latin Quarter at a place called the Chicken Inn. It was owned by the guy who owned Four Roses whiskey. When that job was finished I went to Washington, D.C., with Sidney to play the Brown Derby. Some guys wanted Sidney and I to come to New York and go on the air with Louis Armstrong. But Sidney said he was as big a name as Louis, so Louis could come to Washington. Joe Glaser wouldn't go for that, and we didn't get the job.

When I finally got back to New York I went on the *This Is Jazz* show for Rudi Blesh. They sent to Chicago for Baby Dodds. He came out and him and I worked on the show for almost its whole time on the air. We had guys like Armstrong, Bechet, Muggsy Spanier, Wild Bill Davison, George Brunies, Jimmy Archey, and a whole gang of guys. That's how Jimmy got to be known. He played on the show for a long time. There were a lot of good trumpet players around Harlem in those days. When we first started we'd try to get them to go on, but they'd say they didn't want to play that old-time stuff. After Baby, Jimmy, and I started doing so well, the same guys would come around and say, "Hey, Pops, how about cutting me in on that show you're on?" I'd say, "No, man, this is that old-time stuff you don't wanna play."

Baby Dodds was really a good friend of mine, one of the best I've had in a lifetime. We played a whole lot of jobs together. He's also one of the best drummers. He never overplayed his drums. I'd play a little riff and he'd just keep the beat instead of trying to drown me out. Baby used to come around just so he could be with me and was always passin' compliments to me. He used to say to Alma, "I sure do love that old man." I always thought very highly of him.

When Baby and I were working together a lot in New York, we started playing a lot of college jobs. I've been to Columbia, Yale, Princeton, and lost my teeth at Penn State. I got so drunk I dropped them in the toilet and flushed them before I knew what happened. It was when I was with the college kids I started to drink whiskey heavy. Before that I drank and even got drunk sometimes, but with the college kids, every one of them wanted to buy you a drink. They seemed to be so crazy about me, I couldn't say no. So if there were 25 kids, I'd try to have 25 drinks.

When I did get drunk, I didn't do anyone any harm. Mostly I'd want to sleep, play music, or try to cut up and be funny. I think colored musicians mostly drank booze and the white guys started taking dope. Some young colored musicians did start taking dope after that. The only real trouble I ever had in my life was the drinking I did around New York, and that was all harm to myself.

One time I remember we went over to Rhode Island to play a college date—Jimmy Archey, Art Hodes, me, and a couple of other guys. Art brought a whole suitcase full of whiskey. We all got pretty well loaded, but Art couldn't even stand up. It was wintertime, so we took him outside and laid him out in a snowbank to cool him off. We forgot him. When we finally remembered him, he was nearly frozen stiff. It took us a long time to thaw him out; we worked on it all the way back to New York. He lived, so I guess it didn't do him too much harm.

Another time a bunch of us were playing a boat job on the Hudson River. There were Marty Marsala, Baby Dodds, Albert Nicholas, James P., and myself. Marty and I were drinking up a storm that night, and we kept passing glasses of whiskey up to the boat pilot all night. He got pretty drunk, and when we came into the pier that night he missed his shot and rammed it. James P.'s piano stool broke and James P. came down on his butt. He just sat there smoking his cigarette and all of us laughing. The pilot backed up and then rammed the pier again before he made it.

Baby Dodds and me used to have some wild times in those days. Baby and I used to drive downtown in his car and then get so drunk we'd lose the car. We'd have to sober up so we could go down all the streets looking for it. Drinking sure makes you act funny. Alma has never asked me about money and has always been the best of wives. One night I came home from a gig with the money they'd paid me. I told Alma she was getting too smart so I was going to hide my money. I set a mousetrap and put my money in it in a drawer, so if Alma tried to take it she'd get caught. When I woke up the next day I asked her to give me some money. She said I didn't give her none. I remembered hiding my money but I forgot about the mousetrap. I stuck my hand to get it and nearly got a couple of broken fingers.

In 1948 I made my first trip to Europe with Mezz Mezzrow. Before I could go I had to go to the doctor to get an okay. He told me to lay off the whiskey for 15 days. I went back after 15 days and told him I'd laid off the stuff. He said I'd live a lot longer if I never touched it again. I said, "I quit," and I haven't touched it since. Alma didn't think I'd make it, but I did. In 1959 when my ticker started kicking up, I quit cigarettes.

Before I left New York in about 1954 I was down talking to Spool Head Clarence Williams at his pawnshop on 125th Street between

Fifth Avenue and Lennox Avenue. He was the only colored man in the country to have a pawnshop at that time. I used to go down there to talk to him sometimes. This time I was saying, "There was one band I'd like to come to New York and play, and that was Clairborne Williams's band, my cousin."

Clarence said, "What do you mean, your cousin?"

I said, "My cousin, man; they sure ain't your cousins even with your name." He said, "They were my cousins. All of the family was musical, I even had an aunt who had three young kids that played. I always wondered what happened to them." I said, "You're looking at one of them!" Clarence said, "I been knowing you for over 40 years since New Orleans, and I didn't even know that. Why didn't you make yourself known?" I said, "Why didn't you make yourself known?"

We had a big laugh and talk about finding out we were related after all those years.

Around Harlem and Chicago's South Side all the white people used to come for entertainment. They used to leave their car and walk around from spot to spot. They don't do that anymore; they're scared to even come around. I'm even afraid to walk around those places at night now. In 1955 I took five dollars and went out to get Alma some medicine. As soon as I hit the end of the steps, two doped-up kids grabbed me and choked me till I passed out. They took the five dollars and my cigarettes. Both of them were from the neighborhood, and I knew them. I figured I was lucky to be alive and I'd better get out of Harlem, so I came out here to California to join Earl Hines at the Club Hangover. We had a nice bunch of guys there. Muggsy, Darnell Howard, Ory, sometimes; Earl, Zutty, and other guys.

Earl Hines really knew a lot about music. He taught me more about music than anybody else. He would show me chords I didn't know existed and how you could fit so many different chords together. He's great. Muggsy and I were great friends. The thing he liked to do most was come over and eat Alma's red beans and rice. He was always asking Alma to cook some up for him. The last time he was here he ate two serving bowls full.

A lot of the old guys are gone now. There's only a couple of us left. Montudie and I are about the only ones. I've played with a lot of guys in my life and had a lot of good times. Most of the guys I've played with the last 35 years think I'm a lot older than I am. They remember I played with Freddie Keppard, Manuel Perez, Joe Oliver, and guys like that. That makes you old in their eyes. Some of them think I'm about 150 years old. Well, when I started I was always the youngest one in the band, and now I'm always the oldest. It's been kicks.

Epilogue

On October 30, 1969, at about 3:00 P.M., at 77 years and a few months, George Murphy "Pops" Foster quit the scene. That was the day after I finished the Foreword to this book. After a long illness, Pops died of complications due to blood clots, a tumor found in his stomach, and a weak heart that just gave out. Pops was the kindest, gentlest man I have ever known. I know of no one who has ever spoken against Pops. With me he was tops.

Pops died knowing his life story had been written. I had only the chronology and some of the pictures to go over with him for some final data. Most of the chapters had been delivered to him, and the final four were on the way to the typist when he died. He had read most of the chapters and had said, "It sounds great, just the way I told it." He had misgivings about two items—meeting the woman at George Hooker's house and Jelly's left hand. I told him if he would like, I would pull them out. He said, "They were the truth, so leave them in, and I didn't call the woman's name anyway."

Some will claim that Pops says some nasty things about Armstrong, Jelly, Bechet, and others. He always thought Armstrong and Bechet were great musicians, and he liked Jelly. When he discussed them it was as a friend. There is nothing said in these pages Pops probably had not told the people to their faces. He had such an elfish way of saying things, they never sounded cruel or nasty.

On October 30, 1969, the world lost a great jazzman and I lost a close friend. I would like to say what Baby Dodds said about him: I loved that old man.

—Tom Stoddard

201

Chronology of Musical Groups, 1899–1969

෴

Below is a list of the principal music groups with whom Pops Foster played during this lifetime. Pops and I had not completed the chronology when he passed away. In the book he does not refer to some of the groups listed in the chronology. These are, however, groups he mentioned to me in conversation prior to his death. The list is not all inclusive, since there were numerous other groups he played with occasionally. For example, he toured Europe with the Mezz Mezzrow Orchestra in 1948, Jimmy Archey in 1952, and Sammy Price in 1955. These were really pickup groups for the tours or, in the case of the Archey trip, they were to play with local groups. In some cases where I have put "gigged" (played specific performances), Pops may have played with the group regularly for a month or so, but I am unaware of a permanent connection. In other cases, like the Tuxedo Orchestra, Pops gigged with them for many years before he finally took a regular job.

Wyatt Foster Band, McCall Plantation, Louisiana; 1899–1900
The Fosters, McCall Plantation, Louisiana; 1900–1902
Pickup groups and string trios at lawn parties and fish fries, New Orleans, Louisiana; 1902–1906
Rozelle Orchestra, New Orleans, Louisiana; 1906–1908
Magnolia Orchestra, New Orleans, Louisiana; 1908–1912
Frankie Dusen's Eagle Band, New Orleans, Louisiana; 1908–1910 (gigged)
Kid Ory Band, New Orleans, Louisiana; 1908–1920 (gigged)
Manuel Perez Band, New Orleans, Louisiana; 1908–1915 (gigged)
Freddie Keppard's Olympia Orchestra, New Orleans, Louisiana; 1908–1909 (gigged)
Silver Leaf Band, New Orleans, Louisiana; 1910–1912 (gigged)
Bab Frank's Peerless Orchestra, New Orleans, Louisiana; 1910–1920 (gigged)

202

Hamp Benson's Primrose Orchestra, New Orleans, Louisiana; 1910–1911 (gigged)
Gold Leaf Band, New Orleans, Louisiana; 1910–1912 (gigged)
Jack Carey's Crescent Band, New Orleans, Louisiana; 1909–1915 (gigged)
Toots Johnson Band, Baton Rouge, Louisiana; 1911–1912 (gigged)
Edward Clem Band, New Orleans, Louisiana; 1911–1912 (gigged)
Alphonse Picou Orchestra, New Orleans, Louisiana; 1912–1915 (gigged)
Tuxedo Orchestra, New Orleans, Louisiana; 1912–1920
Thornton Blue Band, New Orleans, Louisiana; 1912–1913 (gigged)
John Robichaux Orchestra, New Orleans, Louisiana; 1912–1913 (gigged)
Dutrey Brothers Band, ship to British Honduras; 1914
Buddy Petit Band, New Orleans, Louisiana; 1915
Tig Chambers Band, New Orleans, Louisiana; 1915–1916 (gigged)
Armand Piron Orchestra, New Orleans, Louisiana; 1915–1917
Amos Riley Band, New Orleans, Louisiana; 1917 (gigged)
The Jazz Syncopators (Fate Marable and the Streckfus Lines), SS *Belle of the Bend*, New Orleans, Louisiana; 1917–1918
Fate Marable and His Jazz Maniacs, SS *Capitol*; 1919–1921
Charlie Creath's Jazz-O-Maniacs, SS *St. Paul*, Mississippi River and at St. Louis, Missouri; 1921, 1923–1925
Eddie Allen's Gold Whispering Band, Mississippi River; 1921
Ory's Sunshine Orchestra, Los Angeles, California; 1922
Curtis Mosby Band, Los Angeles, California; 1922 (gigged)
Oran "Hot Lips" Page Band, Los Angeles, California; 1922 (recorded)
Dewey Jackson's Peacock Orchestra, St. Louis, Missouri; 1925, 1928–1929
Sidney Desvignes Orchestra, New Orleans, Louisiana; 1926–1927
Mutt Carey's Liberty Syncopators, Los Angeles, California; 1927–1928
Elks Brass Band, Los Angeles, California to Chicago, Illinois; 1928
Luis Russell and His Orchestra, New York, New York; 1929–1935
Duke Ellington Orchestra, New York, New York, and Philadelphia, Pennsylvania; 1931 (gigged)
Fletcher Henderson Orchestra, New York, New York; 1931–1933 (gigged)
Horace Henderson Orchestra, New York, New York; 1931–1933 (gigged)
Fats Waller and His Buddies (and his Rhythm), New York, New York; 1929–1935 (recorded and gigged)
Jelly Roll Morton Orchestra, New York, New York; 1932–1935 (rehearsed)
Willie the Lion Smith Band, New York, New York; 1933–1945 (recorded and rehearsed)
Louis Armstrong and His Orchestra, home base New York, New York, but traveled all over U.S.; 1935–1940
Benny Goodman Orchestra, Chicago, Illinois; 1937 (recorded)
Mezz Mezzrow Orchestra, Chicago, Illinois; 1941 (recorded)
James P. Johnson Orchestra, New York, New York; 1942–1955 (gigged)
Pickup groups and various musicians in New York; 1940–1955
Pops Foster Band, New York, New York; 1944
Sidney Bechet Band, Boston, Massachusetts, Washington D.C., and New York, New York; 1945–1948
This Is Jazz house band, New York, New York; 1947–1948
Earl Hines's Club Hangover Orchestra, San Francisco, California; 1955–1960
Pickup groups, concerts, and one-night gigs; 1960–1969

Selected Discography

❧

The following recordings were available on CD in late 2004. Many of these discs, plus related titles, can be ordered at www.jazzbymail.com and www.louisianamusicfactory.com.

Pops Foster performances on CD:

With Henry "Red" Allen
1929–1933, Jazz Chronological Classics

With Jimmy Archey
Dr. Jazz Series (volumes 4 and 13), Jazzology

With Lil Hardin Armstrong
Chicago: The Living Legends—Lil Hardin Armstrong and Her Orchestra, Original Jazz Classics

With Louis Armstrong
1929–1940, ASV Living Era

With Sidney Bechet
Jazz Nocturne (volumes 1–5), Jazz Crusade

With Charlie Creath's Jazz-O-Maniacs
Jazz in Saint Louis, 1924–1927, Timeless

With Wild Bill Davison
Wild Bill Davison's World Famous Jazz Band and Jazzologists, Jazzology
    with Earl Hines
Chicago: The Living Legends—A Monday Date, Original Jazz Classics

With Art Hodes
George "Pops" Foster with Art Hodes, American Music

With Mezz Mezzrow
King Jazz Volume 1: The Mezzrow/Bechet Quintet/Septet, Storyville

With Tony Parenti
Tony Parenti and His New Orleanians, Jazzology

With Luis Russell
1930–1934, Melodie Jazz Classic

With the *This Is Jazz* house band
This Is Jazz, The Historic Broadcasts of Rudi Blesh (seven volumes), Jazzology.
Volume 3 features Louis Armstrong; Leadbelly appears on *Volume 5*.

With various artists
World's Greatest Jazz Concert #1, Jazzology. The band includes George Brunies, Baby Dodds, Muggsy Spanier, Art Hodes, and "Hot Lips" Page.
John Reid Collection, American Music. Features Peter Bocage, Louis Nelson, Alphonse Picou, Walter Decou, Sidney Bechet, Louis Keppard, and Paul Barbarin.

Other New Orleans–style jazz recordings:

Louis Armstrong
Hot Five and Sevens, JSP

Sidney Bechet
Young Sidney Bechet, Timeless

Baby Dodds
Baby Dodds, American. Includes several Dodds narratives on New Orleans style and drum performance.

Johnny Dodds
Great Original Performances 1923–1929, Louisiana Red Hot

Bunk Johnson
Bunk Johnson and His Superior Jazz Band, Good Time Jazz

Freddie Keppard
The Complete Set 1923–1926, Retrieval

George Lewis
Jazz Funeral in New Orleans, Tradition

Jelly Roll Morton
1923–1924, Milestone

King Oliver
King Oliver and His Creole Jazz Band, 1923, Melodie Jazz Classic

Original Dixieland Jazz Band
First Jazz Recording 1917–1923, EPM Musique

Kid Ory
1922–1945, Classics

Various artists
Recorded in New Orleans (volumes 1 and 2), Good Time Jazz
Recorded in New Orleans 1925–1928, Jazz Oracle. Tracks by the bands of Sam Morgan and Papa Celestin.

Selected Bibliography

Asbury, Herbert. *The French Quarter*. New York: Alfred Knopf, 1936.

Blesh, Rudi, and Harriet Janis. *They All Played Ragtime*. New York: Oak, 1966.

Charters, Samuel. *The Bluesmen*. New York: Oak, 1967.

———. *The Country Blues*. New York: Holt, Rinehart and Winston, 1959.

———. *The Poetry of the Blues*. New York: Oak, 1963.

Feather, Leonard. *Encyclopedia of Jazz*. New York: Horizon, 1960.

Hentoff, Nat, and Albert MacCarthy. *Jazz*. New York: Rinehart and Co., 1959.

Hodeir, Andre. *Jazz: Its Evolution and Essence*. New York: Grove, 1956.

Schuller, Gunther. *Early Jazz*. New York: Oxford University Press, 1968.

Stearns, Marshall. *The Story of Jazz*. New York: Oxford University Press, 1956.

Ulanov, Barry. *A History of Jazz in America*. New York: Viking, 1952.

Index

207

CPSIA information can be obtained at www.ICGtesting.com
Printed in the USA
BVOW04s1704290714

360892BV00005B/8/P